MW01603140

BEST POETS OF 2023

VOL. 2

John T. Eber Sr.

MANAGING EDITOR

A publication of

Eber & Wein Publishing

Pennsylvania

Library of Congress
Cataloging in Publication Data

ISBN 978-1-60880-771-0

Proudly manufactured in the United States of America by

Eber & Wein Publishing

Pennsylvania

Best Poets of 2023

Havisham Time

I remember that night when she walked into Joe's.
At that time of year,
the clock stopped at twenty-to-nine,
just like my heart.

All tightly wrapped in what remained of a wedding dress,
yellow stained silk and lace,
it had a tattered veil hanging out of her greying matted hair.

She had an odd walk, and I was sure she lost a shoe along the way.

Bony fingers pointed around the bar, covered with
tarnished jewelry and ending in broken nails.
She had a crumpled old piece of paper clutched in her hand,
and I could tell she was all business.

When she passed my steel barstool, I caught a whiff of something,
and it wasn't Christian Dior.

She dragged a stool beside me, and the bartender, Arthur,
asked if she wanted something.
She just hissed at him through clenched teeth.

Then she leaned in close to me and whispered,
"Do you feel like you have lost her?"
She placed a pencil on the bar in front of me.
And all I could do was stare into my empty glass.

Danny Brookhart
Scottsdale, AZ

Precious Memories

Our memories of Mom and Dad reach back in time....

They had many things to say
As they taught us to grow and learn along the way

We hold tight to precious memories of summer days
As we worked with Dad picking rocks and baling hay

We remember Mom on beautiful summer nights
On the swing as she enjoyed stars shining bright

Sometimes when life got difficult and gray
They would work even harder so the bills they could pay

They both stood strong with encouragement on the day
Each of their children moved away

In times of trouble they told us to pray
To trust in God that everything would be okay

We see them in our precious memories every day
Oh how we wish God would have let them stay
For one more day

We love and miss you, Mom and Dad

Donna Everly-Anderson
Baxter, MN

The Mountain

If the mountain seems too high today
then climb a hill, instead
If the morning brings you sadness
it's okay to stay in bed
If the day ahead weighs heavy
and your plans feel like a curse
there's no shame in rearranging
don't make yourself feel worse
If a shower stings like needles
and a bath feels like you'll drown
If you haven't washed your hair today
don't throw away your crown
A day is not a lifetime
A test is not defeat
Don't think of it as failure
just a quiet, calm retreat
It's okay to take a moment
from an anxious fractured mind
The world will not stop turning
while you go get realigned
The mountain will still be there
when you want to try again
You can climb it in your own time
just be patient until then

Caren Morris
Atkins, AR

Silent Tears

Silent tears I cried for you, he said. For I never got to know you.
Conceived under the stars and the heavens above.
For my life ended without taking a look at your face, or a goodbye.
Now in your dreams, I come to you.
Look at my eyes, a reflection of yourself you'll see.
More tears came as we both shared silent tears.
I tightly held his hand, but like a cloud, he disappeared from whence he came.
I cried in silence, regardless of the time gone by.
My father came to visit me and put my heart at ease!

Ursula L. Bennett
Albuquerque, NM

Mixed Tapes

The best of all great escapes
Bittersweet emotional landscapes
Perfect places captured in time
Soulful phases I can always rewind
Friendly faces of memories that will forever live on
Mixed tapes of times when friendships and love remain strong
I can always replay
Where the magical moments of you will always stay
I will be waiting for you, too

Daniel Brian Sherman
Binghamton, NY

"In Memory of Me"
Just Press Play...

Seasons

Seasons come and go and pass like the
wind and goes by along with time.
Spring comes with flowers that grow
and with rain. Summer is hot and muggy;
people love to go for a swim plus eat
snowballs plus ice cream to cool off.
When fall begins leaves start to fall
and school starts back. Then when winter
comes it turns cold and begins to snow.
It goes by with time before you
know it starts all over again.
People change just like the wind but
seasons start over again and again.
Fall has windy days where summer ends.
Plus winter with snow children love
to play and throw snowballs in the snow.

Rickey Ethridge
Meridian, MS

Memories of My Sister

When the rain falls
I think of you
When the flowers bloom
I think of you
When the sun shines
I think of you
When I see frolicking kittens
I think of you
When there's a breeze
When there's laughter
When I feel sad
When I feel glad
All the things
That we went through
Will always make me
   Think of you
I love and miss you DeeDee

Suzan Doll
Hawthorne, NV

Womankind

The Fisher of Men
The woman cried out
Lovingly to the man
Touching his shoulderFollow Me
I'm the Fisher of Men
The woman whispered
seductively to the man
Touching his chestFollow Me
She's the Fisher of Men
The woman's breath hissed
Kiss me to the man
Touching his lipsFollow Me
God warned me
About that kind of woman,Me?
The Fisher of Men

Julie Uecker
Menifee, CA

Suitcase, Boxes, and Bags

Suitcase, boxes, and bags. Never having what I
needed, just making due with what I had.
Pictures on canvas, paintings all upon my
walls and the ones at a stand still lurk in the
silent halls.
Feelings of heartbreak, feelings of glee, all
the feelings are wrapped up with a ribbon of
happiness of the love you shared with me.
I long for the sweet and simple times when
never feared the day where you were no
longer mine. I'd give anything to go back to
that space in time.
Suitcase, boxes, and bags. Never having what
I needed, just making due with what I had.
Secrets that shared memories we hold ever
so dear. Life is not the same without you there.
Roads are long and lonely. All I could hope
for is our paths will cross in time again and
these suitcases, boxes, and bags will be
emptied and put way to put a smile on your
face and make new memories that will never change.

Rhonda Leigh Van Camp
Follansbee, WV

A Season of Golden Dreams

Immense feelings of a valley so high
Relinquishes itself on an unspoken cry.
A tear intertwines with a feeling of hope
To diminish the journey of a downward hidden slope.

Many trials upon a hidden sky
Bring love to the answer of a meaningful reply.
Memories camoflauge the betrayal of a song
Brings to the present where the story belongs.

A chapter creates a season of golden dreams
Emptying itself of unruly hidden schemes.

A partner holds the key to her success,
Having a moment in time to open the rest.

Colleen S. Johnson
Salisbury, MD

Choose

When our mind reveals our soul
　It ends up not the same.
Instead of knowing what it was
　It's what we choose to name.

When our eyes reflect our view
　The signs may not agree.
Instead of looking like it did
　It's what we choose to see.

When the song of life appears
　Its voice may not be clear.
Instead of sounding like itself
　It's what we choose to hear.

When you search for who you are
　Include what's wise and free.
Instead of being what we were
　We're what we choose to be.

John C. Cook
North Palm Beach, FL

Grandparents, Moms, Dads of the World

You are making us fearful
You cause us to be tearful
We ponder and wonder why
You "pave" many ways for us to die
No love for us youths in the world
Supporting "bad actors" harm boys and girls
You of "no color" were taught, "I'm superior"
Motivating you to treat others inferior
Inherited roles made some "big-headed"
Inflicting mistreatment to their own instead
Some elected people "worked" for mankind
Others in office not keeping democracy in mind
Actions of adults are making us mad
To know grandparents, moms, and dads
Are doing things to make us sad
Assuring us a gloomy future that is bad
We know why you cultivate hateful acts
You don't want us to know historical facts
You are selfish and greedy
Not showing Agape love towards the needy
Youths see you serving man
Forgetting a "Higher Power" is in command
We see hypocrisy in what you say and do
Your actions shorten the lives of us youths.

Mamie J. Reynolds
Montgomery, AL

Death's-Head Revisited

It was the darkest period
of the last century—
a period of immeasurable pain,
cruelty of the highest order,
a time when some among us, willingly,
cast aside their very humanity
and walked in step
with the devil himself.
Those who walked in darkness,
bereft of human compassion,
became human monsters,
and where their booted feet landed,
people died.
Upon their caps was a death's-head,
a symbol of authority, of subjugation;
they were perveyers of
a nightmare that never seemed to end.
They were compelled by hate,
by an intense desire to destroy,
to eradicate those they considered inferior.
For years, they practiced their unholy endeavors,
while their evil empire crumbled around them.
Then, mercifully, it all came to an end;
the Third Reich was no more.
Still, it is indeed a pity that the hate they engendered
still remains with us, a dark legacy of intolerance.

Steven M. Lambert
Warsaw, IN

For most of my life, I have been a student of the second World War. One of the most horrible aspects of the war was the liquidation of the Jewish people in countries that the Nazi's had conquered. Such was the magnitude of this atrocity that the survivors are haunted by the horror of what occurred during that time to this day. May the good Lord grant that such things never happen again. And may God give the survivors peace.

No Expired Prayer

Your glory is splenderful, no other can compare
Always loyal Lord thy presence is always near, always there.
From heaven's throne, you hear all pleas, our sorrows,
you endure Jesus and share.
Remember in Your kingdom, there is never an unanswered or expired prayer.
No matter how long we patiently wait,
No matter how enduring, always in Your heart glow with faith.
There's a line from Heaven, twenty-four hours a day,
Jesus is the operator, never a disconnection, He listens to everything you say.
When times seem to linger, and we think only of ourself,
Without His love, a hollow shell of man would be left.
I'm so thankful, Lord, You're so just, graceful, and fair.
Your power is unique and divine
Your response isn't on my schedule, but on Yours Lord,
Always faithfully on time.
There's always an answer, no matter how heavy the burden is to
share and bear.
He always know, no prayers left unanswered,
No matter how long it takes, you will receive an answered prayer!

Ella R. Dixon
Yazoo City, MS

The Morning Air

The morning air is
crisp and still. All
around me is silence,
the only sound I hear
is the birds flying over
my head, and the cars
driving by. The peace
and quiet is welcoming
to me, and it brings
a smile to my face.

Elizabeth A. Anzalone
South Plainfield, NJ

Your Hand

As I sit here on the bed tonight the only way I can clear my mind is to write.
My heart has been broken since you passed away. Soon it's going to be
a year but it only seems like yesterday. It's so hard to sleep at
night not having your hand holding mine. Are you here to say I love you,
like we did every night. After all these years together who would have ever
thought the two of us one day be apart? So to sleep at night I hold
your picture where I once held your hand in mine.

Elizabeth Bowman
Clintwood, VA

The Wedding Dress

My journey was long
Beginning in 1941.
It was love at first sight;
She knew I was the one.
I felt the love in her touch,
In the way she caressed me.
But soon her touch was gone;
That's the way it had to be.
Often I would be awakened
When I felt her loving hand,
As she once again remembered
The day we looked so grand.
Through the years, as I grew older
And all my memories had been made,
The longing for her tender touch
Had begun to fade.
Then, the touch of other hands
As gentle as before
Caressed me once again;
The love was so much more.
I have again been chosen
To fulfill another's dreams
And although a little older,
It again was as it seemed.

Judith Anne Melvin
Blackwood, NJ

This is about my mother's wedding dress. She had passed away in 2009. Her oldest great-granddaughter got married in 2013. So, my mother's wedding dress was in her hope chest for seventy-two years before Ashleigh wore it. The dress was in excellent condition.

The Wonder of Kelly

Curled sleeping like down against my breast
Innocence reigning supreme
Your hair flowing softly over my arm
I touch the blush of your cheek
Assuming the pose of an angel
Breathlessly serene, at peace in your dreams
But I surmise you walk in daylight
Of memories past of a thousand lives
My child of twelve, I pull you closer
Until your heartbeat keeps in rhythm with mine
Clinging possessively to your warmth
Before my mystic moonbeam awakens
From your moment of birth
You walked among the stars, knowing mysteries
We mortals dared not imagine
Chamolean and illusive like a rainbow
Dancing in the meadows you mesmerized us
With your secrecy casting your spell
Weaving fantasies supreme in your knowledge
You taunt our imaginations
Leaving us to wonder
Are you a child of our conception?
Or a gift of immortality...

Donna J. Shaver
Laurens, NY

This poem is dedicated to my daughter Kelly Pinter who lives in Laurens, NY. I wrote this one night when she was twelve years old and we were lying on the bed together watching TV. She was always a mysterious and delightful child. She grew to be an intelligent, talented, beautiful, amazing woman. She gives me great comfort in my old age.

Love Unsaid

Your scent still on me
Mixing with the essences of gifts
Your caring called from me,
And you, your longing fulfilled,
Secure, adream, I woke to thoughts
More wide and wise than all the truths
Our fleshless insight yields
And all to this reduce:
That living simply is loving too
While living true to guides without
Leads nowhere but to fictions
Only hatred can support.
And so to me your love is like
The flash of flowers in a field
And like those, too, your hands have nursed,
A lamp unto the dark night of my soul.

Gary F. Seifert
Falls Church, VA

Remember Me

God has given me a great life,
One with faith and love.
Now I am in Heaven,
In the beautiful home above.

Now I know how much I'm loved.
I've waited all my life.
My future is eternal,
I'll have no pain or strife.

I love my family and friends.
They've been so kind to me.
And now that I'm in Heaven,
Their kindness I shall see.

Photography was my career.
My awards are such a treasure.
For Aerospace, I traveled some,
For me it was a pleasure.

I know I'm always in God's heart.
His love is here to see.
And now to my family and friends,
I say 'Remember Me.'

Sharon E. Olmos
Huntington Beach, CA

The Dahm of Stress Valley

The weary dahm struggled with all her might
To hold the raging water tight

Suddenly was heard a dreadful shriek
As in the dahm, there sprang a leak

Villagers scrambled to higher ground
As the feeble dahm came crashing down

Soon there was peace all around
But many villagers were drowned

The villagers gathered to count their cost
Buried their loved ones and mourned their loss

Their dam, now a tower against the sky
The little valley will never die

2 Corinthians 12:10

Connie L. Wood
Park Forest, IL

I was suddenly, forcefully removed from my family when I was five years old. I had so many unanswered questions. What have I done? Why is Mommy crying? Where am I going? It was about a year later when four of us were reunited with our father. Where is Mom? It was later when I learned about nervous breakdowns and divorce. Eventually, I found out my younger brother and younger, mentally disabled sister were living elsewhere. Our father was so abusive that my brothers and sister left as soon as they could. I was determined to graduate from high school. Suddenly, forcefully I left and stayed with my older brother and his wife for about two months till I graduated from high school. A few years later, I joined the navy. I married a selfish man who caused our family emotional and financial distress. He divorced me in 1996 to marry one of many mistresses. Currently, I am still happily single and hoping to reunite with my three children. Physically, emotionally, and spiritually I am seventy-five years old. I have made many mistakes, but I am comforted in the knowledge of God's forgiveness.

I Have a Talk with Jesus

I have a talk with Jesus
When things are going wrong
And He will always listen
To Jesus I belong.

He knows all things about me
My needs He does fulfill
I trust in what He tells me
He says, "Peace, peace be still"

For He's my Lord and Savior
Our Father's precious Son
And He will solve all problems
Yes every single one.

His peace is always with me
He is my guiding light
So I have a talk with Jesus
And all things turn out right.

Alma M. Gaines
New Rochelle, NY

Johnny My Brother

Johnny we nicknamed you redbeard.
You thought that was really cool.
You liked to pretend you were Santa.
Johnny my brother, this is very true.
You loved to have people laugh in many ways.
Johnny if only others knew you
And your funny ways.
Many mistook your tactics of words in different ways.
You only wanted laughter, and many turned away.
Johnny I always tried to protect you,
Even in your early days.
It was harder in your aging days.
Now you can perform for Jesus for He knows
Your sweet, sweet spirit.
You can sit and run and play with trucks
And cars with all the Heavenly children.
Johnny it's so sad you had to leave us.
But you did go when you were called.
Jesus will be with you, taking you in his plan.
I know you'll be okay now.
You're in Jesus's hands.
I love you, little brother.
Guard us with your love.

Rita E. Bean
Pittsfield, MA

Issues

The heart of a whippoorwill
beats sadly through the night's chill.
Faith denied his mother's care;
Issues are his cross to bear.
Few qualifies to boost pride
and teach a soul how to fly.

Donna C. Whittemore
Gadsden, AL

Patch to Pan

With the feel and smell of autumn in the air
and beautiful leaves scattered here and there

Pick a pumpkin from the patch with autumn's warm flare
and think of the wonderful dishes you could prepare

The pumpkin's skin is hard to peel, to chop, and to slash
but easy to cook and easy to mash

With pumpkin and spice and everything nice
why not make a pie, some bread, and cheesecake tonight?

Bon Appetit

Florace G. Hensley
Titusville, FL

Peace

What has peace done not to be loved
Who did peace kill
Who has peace disrespected
Is peace a form of neglect
Is peace doing nothing
Is peace causing loneliness
Is peace nothing but also a blessing

Everett E. Draper
Toledo, OH

Unmask the Charade

Your words rang and rippled
Leaving my youthful body completely crippled
I'm unable to walk away.

My emotions nearly tripled
Beautiful truths now riddled
I'm holding onto a dead bouquet.

Our hearts were as one
Our story had just begun
Your adoration was pretend.

Your web has been spun
My world has been undone
All love lost in the end.

Michelle Leanne Corbin
Novato, CA

My Friend

Everything you say and do
Makes laughter with you very good.
It makes me happy that I know you
Keeps me smiling as it should.

If you should ever go away
I know I would just sit and cry,
For my friend who left one day
Without even telling me goodbye.

You always make me laugh or smile
As only you really know how.
It might be for only a little while
And I do enjoy it so much for now.

To you I send this through the mail;
In a couple of days you will read.
With you things will never fail;
Your presence in my life is all I need.

So this poem I finally do give
With my friendship and love to you,
Hoping our friendship will always live,
For I would be lost without you.

Jerry T. Freeman
Lake City, AR

Ripperology

Jack the Ripper
 who was he
 Chapman, Pizer
 Kosminski

Man or woman
 Polish or Jew
 gentry, lover
 vicar, gumshoe

Opened them up
 Sternum to thigh
 Tabram, Nichols
 Elizabeth Stride

Someone knew
 refused to tell
 Jack the Ripper
 cackles from Hell

Marcia Ausema
Grand Rapids, MI

Looking Back on My Life Today

Looking back on my life today
In the most extraordinary way
Reflecting on happy moments long ago
And the tough times that went by so slow
I close my eyes and go back in time
To the innocence and happiness that was mine
Life was simple and filled with so much love
How did it turn and become so rough?
The pictures in the albums and in my mind
Bring me back to those wonderful times
As a child so young and care-free
To the teenager that I longed to be
And then I was married and gained a spouse
And we created a "home" in our little house
Then children soon were a part of our life
And a family we became with so much pride
We lost many loved ones along the way
As we began to age from day to day
And now I sit pondering the memories
Of what was then and what the future holds for me
We have followed a long and winding road
Some of us have carried quite a heavy load
But we stand tall and proud and keep moving on
With the rise of the sun at each and every dawn

Cordelia Silvestri
Ossining, NY

SUNFLOWERS

Sunflowers grow tall and sway in the breeze.
Until their petals fall and centers become seeds.
Nature summons the sun to dry and to shine!
Feathered friends of flight like to stop in to dine.
Local bird feeders all around town
Open 24/7 morning through dawn.
Winds may blow and winter freeze, yet
Everybody I know enjoys watching them eat!
Rules of recycling, sharing, and good tweets
Seem to work well from their little beaks!

Barbara J. Ravanelli
Milwaukee, WI

We are joined by nature and can find comfort in knowing—if God can provide for His little creatures...He can for us, too! I, too, believe!

The Modern Pacifier

It's not tied to a ribbon around a baby's neck,
But they are everywhere and can cause a wreck.
If you don't have one people are simply amazed,
Because they are in a sort of high tech daze.
It's the technical advance of modern time,
Usually sparkling clean but can have some grime.
They are found in a holster, back pocket or purse,
And maybe even the last ride in a hearse.
It does wonderous things so some people say,
I don't really know but what the hey.
It can track you from near and far,
Even if you are at the local bar.
You can ask it a question and get an answer back,
And hopefully it will put you on the right track.
Wanna play a game, that's possible, too,
Nobody else needed, it's just for you.
By now you have probably figured it out,
It's the cell phone, without a doubt.

Fred Resler
Bosque Farms, NM

Everywhere you go people are on their phones, they will bump into you because they are looking at it and you think that a person is talking to you but, as usual, they are on their phone.

Today I Am 80 Years Old/Just Yesterday

I was born during WWII. Dad was in the army
Dad came home, started building our house
I was 6, jumping to reach the pump handle in the yard
We had an outhouse, one car, I have two sisters
Big cook stove in the kitchen, coal bin in the basement
I played jacks, hopscotch, marbles, hide and seek
I helped Mom snap beans, shell peas to freeze
Dad drove tractor and trailer, I picked corn
I was running to catch the school bus to read and write
I danced to the 45 rpm records in the basement
I went rollerskating, walked to see friends
Our phone on the wall, 3 party lines, no area code
Breadman, milkman, Fuller Brush man came to our door
I learned to drive, got engaged, graduated, got a job
I got married, bought a house monthly payment $57.50
I had two children, cloth diapers, rubber pants
Wringer washer, no clothes dryer, hung clothes outside
My kids are grown up already, graduated and married
I have five grandchildren, now two great-grandchildren
I am divorced, my parents are gone, and also one sister
Life has many ups and downs, sad times, happy times
Yesterday life was so different, life was good
Yesterday I worked hard, learned all I could, years pass
I am happy I grew up yesterday in the country
Yesterday made me who I am today, I am thankful
I am blessed for today I turn 80 years old!

Anita L. Rogers
Royersford, PA

I have been so blessed in my journey turning eighty years old. I have met so many amazing people along the way. Many have become forever friends. However, each person who has traveled through my life has taught me some life lesson. Everyone who crossed my path was for a reason only God knows. I am so grateful and thankful for each person who has helped me along the way leaving footprints. Life's journey is an open book. We fill the pages each day making memories. Each new day an unknown adventure. Love and hugs to Andrew and Shelley.

Scrapbook

While Jim waits—happy, patient,
Dad puts together
A big "JFK" scrapbook,
As he sits at desk,
In corner of living room,
In late evenings after dark.
Many articles
From newspapers, magazines
He tapes them all in,
Along with many pictures
And writes down quotes as well,
Gunsmoke on TV.
Grandfather clock ticks to left,
And lamp shines to right.
With nicknack shelf up above,
Pens, pencils, papers in drawers,
For many evenings
Of smart and careful research.
After many months,
Dad puts scrapbook together,
Smiles at great accomplishment,
Hands his gift to Brother Jim.

William D. Irwin
Princeton, IL

I dedicate this poem in loving memory to my brother Jim and our father Tom "Red" Irwin (who loved football, were hard workers, and were great family men). I also dedicate this poem in thankful appreciation to everyone who helped me become a locally-published author (including Grandma Estella Palmer, Aunt Betty Irwin, Sweetheart Krystal, Barbara, Dave, Joe, Mary, Sue, Scott, Tina, Debbie, Edith, Shirley, Cliff, all writing group friends, and especially Lord Jesus Himself).

Don't Get Cocky Driving a Convertible

Man driving convertible feeling he's on top of the world. The convertible's top is down just because it feels good. He didn't stop at the edge of the parking lot to see if another automobile was coming down Main Street. He just drove straight out onto Main Street. BANG! The car coming smashed right into the convertible, sending it back into the parking lot. It came out of doing a full circle with the driver's head whipping around looking like a town clown. The driver of the convertible was cocksure, brash, hasty, impudent, arrogant, and conceited.

Michael G. Anderson
Tewksbury, MA

This poem is a true story. On Main Street in Tewksbury, MA, my father and I drove by a car accident as it was happening. I said "Oh" in shock and my father said, "He wasn't watching where he was going." I want to update everybody. In a past Eber & Wein book I wrote I have two nieces. It's the year 2024 and I now have three nieces. One of my nieces gave birth to a girl. Besides the year 2012, my female cousin gave birth in the year 2015. I hope everybody will have a good day.

God Is Listening

People talk of what hurts
What happened to the world
What happened to people who
really care
What happened to truth and trust
God is listening
People lost everything; we turn
our back on them
People pray, do they? Some are cold
People lost faith
God is listening
We need hope, truth
We need to listen to each other
We need help and understanding
We need to kneel and pray for real
For God will be listening
I believe God hears everything
God is listening, just pray

Dianne Hill
Morris, IL

Latria

Tell that old fox: casting out devils and curing the
sheep is done today and tomorrow but on the
    3rd day the Lamb will be perfected
Now a martyr's predestinated path has been
    miraculously redirected (Rev. 6:9-11)
To actually follow in the footsteps of the Master
    resurrected
Eden's osteopathic moral perversion has now
    been corrected

This infinite and most gracious accomplishment
    is purely diametric
With the pharisee's forceful manipulative grip all are
    considered a lowly, doleful dialectic
They can distinguish the jots and titles but their
    disastrous' doctrinal is diacaustic
Witness as the most Holy Scripture quaintly empties into
    a new diastolic

The ultimate supreme worship offered only to God alone
    by those He pre-selected
If then: the whole of your life will be totally affected
Looking up to austere heights awaiting the orthotropic
    spiritual growth, as directed
Falling down on your face not accepting this discursive
    dianoetic stance of being rejected

Jeffrey L. White
Elkhorn, WI

At the Sound of Your Voice

At the sound of Your voice, You created all things,
With the music of Heav'n the whole universe sings,
And I join in the song, to praise and adore,
O Jesus, my marvelous Lord!

And I love You, my Lord, and in You I delight,
My Savior, my great endless joy;
And I long for the day when my faith will be sight,
And I'll hear the sweet sound of Your voice!

At the sound of Your voice, those who sleep will awake,
And then we who still live, in a moment be changed,
At the sound of the trumpet, the full cadence of joy,
At the marvelous sound of Your voice!

And I love You, my Lord, and in You I delight,
My Savior, my great endless joy;
And I long for the day when my faith will be sight,
And I'll hear the sweet sound of Your voice!

Joyce Keedy
Towson, MD

Written after playing a chord progression on my autoharp. I extended it, added a melody, and these words. This is the end result. It tells of the unspeakable joy at the sound of my Savior's voice. I look forward to the soon, sure coming of Jesus; in the meantime, it is my great privilege to serve Him as church organist. I first started writing poetry at age ten, playing piano at five, and organ at seventeen. The Lord has given me the words and music; now I rejoice to offer them back to Him. Always, to the glory of God!

The Journey

I woke today from a
subtle dream.
Your hand in mine so soft
and clean.

Just yesterday you said
goodbye.
I did not smile, I did not cry.
On words I did rely.

Your last embrace, stayed like a
song.
Your quiet refrain, "you
did no wrong."

I'll travel on and play
and sing.
Like a pathless bird
without a wing.

Another love will
soon be mine.
I'll wait for her,
and cherish the time.

Joyce H. Pait
Southern Pines, NC

Her Weed of Atomic Wonder

Old disheveld poor alone
Far from help
Empty sky
Barren lawn
Dusty windblown door
Everyone asking why
Association calls
People yell
No one tells them
Go to Hell
In tears each eve
With weathered cane
Out the door she goes
And there in twilight's glow
Blossoms most exquisite she beholds
The wonder of a certain weed
God's gift for grateful poor
Yet, nary a seed glade in the wind
Does she see these days
For her eyes have gone too dim
Still, in her modest musings in the night
God she speaks her thanks
For chance to listen, right to think
And spirit to freely land
An atomic Christ for trouble's end.

David M. Schmidt
Panama City, FL

By God's Design

Tiny little fingers and tiny little toes,
by God's design, His miracles show.
Science can't compete with God's mighty hand;
God's creations appear at His command.
Somewhere out there is a living soul,
ready to be born to someone, it goes.
Where, when, how, our Lord only knows;
a mother and father will cradle it so.
God had in mind to create little ones
to give parents a daughter or a son.
No matter trials parents go thru,
the lengths God goes to create me and you!
Snowflakes are designed each differently,
as God has made the wonderful sky and sea.
You're wondering who created world and man;
God almighty holds the world in His hand.

Sylvia Weakley
Etlan, VA

Jungle Romance

The people in our local village must think we're both crazy because we choose to live like Tarzan and Jane, but we're both of sound mind and body, both quite sane. Maybe Amber and I were meant to be monkeys or birds living in trees, but we're both very much in love, and as happy as can be. I am dazzled by Amber's figure and luscious smile; I like the way she keeps her long red hair, smooth, untangled, and unfurled. Amber to me is the most beautiful woman I've ever known, the most beautiful girl in the world. She has a voice like an angel, soft, melodic, and fair. When she sings it's like music that fills the air. Our lives are primitive, even difficult at times; very few people understand us, or find our reasons for living this way plausible. But we've both found a happiness neither of us thought was possible. We don't have a lot of material things, or special talents, or extraordinary powers, but we have a unique eternal love, a special relationship, a blessing that is truly ours.

Alan Knight
Champaign, IL

Shango

Shango
Orisha of strength
and beauty
God of thunder
God of light

Helper of the weak
Aid of the poor
He was the ever-present
Friend to victims of
the middle passage

He knew who was to
survive to these
hostile shores
He knew who to assist
to the realm of spirit

He knew everything
in life and in death
and was eternally
accompanied by the
wondrous beauty
Riverine Oshun

*Orisha - a great spirit, a god
*Riverine - one living close to and enjoying rivers

Eleanor Shannon Lee Blakeny
New York, NY

My life has become more difficult these last months due to health issues. I am very happy to survive to write a poem for Eber & Wein! Thanks for your invitation!

I Declined

It went by in a flash
do not know how fast,
a bicycle made of glass.
She is so beautiful who is this girl
who rode a bicycle made of glass.
A warm wind blew as she passed.
Her hair whirled in a contrast,
as though a prism were attached.
As fast as she came, she disappeared
and vanished into a grassy clear.
The next morning there did appear
a golden staircase on the clear.
I was invited to climb,
but at this moment I declined.

Dolores Kutzer
Kill Devil Hills, NC

Lil Boy

Lil boy, lil boy
Where are you
I've looked everywhere
In all your favorite places
and can't find you
Lo! I hear the sound of wings
The angels have come
to take you to the Rainbow Bridge
where you'll meet your old friends
I can see you now little tail wagging
as Brandi, Rocky, and Shorty greet you
Be happy, little guy
I have to stay here
The cats need me
But one day, I'll be by
and we'll all go down
that last long trail together

Evelyn Stonesifer
Lecanto, FL

Simply Intrinsic

I'm just sitting here thinking
drinking up the sunshine
music fluctuating the thought waves of my mind
feeling space and time pass on by
with no particular reason or rhyme
Sitting here on cloud nine
just chilling, willing to start a flame
letting my imagination reign
I get so pained with desire that comes with the fire
lighting the flame of my heart
there are many mysterious anomalies and memories
I have yet to figure out they loom in the rooms of my mind
My inquiring mind knows that we are not alone
in this multi-dimensional universe
I find myself gazing at a distant star
and know that it would be the ultimate high
to go on a magic carpet ride throughout the universe
Wondering, how did it all get started?
This question is not for the light-hearted
It may change your perception on how we were created
Extraterrestrials and us were on the cusp of discovery
Everything in the universe has a physic connection
a reflection of all inner sources
So hold on tight we're taking a flight
We will touch the stars and fly amongst the planets to Mars

Jane Schrader
Bay City, MI

My uncle Dr. Richard Muller inspired my poem. He was a world-renouned archaeologist. He worked worldwide with the Smithsonian Institute and was a professor at many universities. He has traveled and studied throughout the world; some of these studies included ancient civilizations and their connection to extraterrestrials. At an early age he sparked my interest in metaphysics and extraterrestrials; these studies have stayed with me to this day.

Air Waves to Heaven

Heaven may seem like millions of miles away
But it is not
No telephone or internet is needed
Voicing invisible air waves to Heaven
Heaven can mean many meanings
Like living in the heart as a residence
Seventh heaven means a state of extreme happiness
The place where God and exalted angels dwell
Can we talk to God?
We talk with God in prayer
Prayers reach Heaven through air waves
They are heard because in the beginning was the Word
The Redeemer intercedes for all at their requests
In thoughts, in speaking out loud, in prayer behests
One great division of the universe
Houses visible stars, sun, moon and planets
Air waves to Heaven applies to a euphemism euphoria
State of well being a good feeling
By giving verbal thanks and praise to God, Jesus Holy Spirit
Blessing the now circumstances
Expecting healings wisdoms, joy, protections
On heaven's air waves two way street
Calling foods, music, places heavenly can comfort
Heaven is also called the firmament
Air waves to Heaven's free open lines are permanent
Rewards for believing are promised by Hebrews eleven

Joan Mays
West Brooklyn, IL

Thank you for this opportunity to write. Writing good words helps people enable themselves, causing advancement of people to continue. What Jesus said about doing the right thing is the greatest inspiration. Having participated in family raising, working in college, agriculture, medical and business careers through the years offered much experience to write poetry about.

Ivy over the Door

You've worked so hard to improve your life
While the ivy grows over the door
Suffering for years since reaching adulthood
While the ivy grows over the door

Fixing all the mistakes, sins from the past
While the ivy grows over the door
Feeling this free soul was trapped in a cast
While the ivy grows over the door

Holding your breath for that special someone
While the ivy grows over the door
Wishing for the meaning in your life to come
While the ivy grows over the door

No matter how precious time is spent
The ivy will still grow
Then your body, heart, and mind will expire
While the ivy grows over the door

Lucas J. Guimond
Fort Edward, NY

Noah

In a world full of danger, violence, and hate,
He lives in a world untainted, how great.
Innocent and living without a single care.
How great it would be if we all lived there.
No sadness or grief in a world that's full of it.
Only joy and happiness in a world in need of it.
God protects him from the bad the world shares.
How great it would be if we all lived there.
Just love to express and hugs every day.
How simple it is to him in every way.
His earth is our Heaven, everywhere.
How great it would be if we all lived there.
God made him special, there is no doubt.
Who are we to question what His plan is about.
The boy is pure love, God's answer to prayer.
How great it would be if we all lived there.

Jennifer D. Payne-Hoover
Benton, KY

Dream State

I'm swimming in the bluest water lake of Canada—
a calming side stroke.
Suddenly people in the water around me,
so much commotion, kicking, disturbing motion.
I wanted nothing but to reach the shore.
Why is that man wearing an aluminum foil hat,
frozen, an ominous stare... then disappeared.
Minutes elapsed—what was the point of that!
"I like this place—my mental state seems clear.
Maybe I can relocate here."
Who are these Australians, these aliens?
I was struck with momentary fear.
Where are the black trash bags?
Have to get rid of these filthy rags.
Desperate searching I located the bags.
How did I get from the blue water to here?
Was it a paid job?... So unclear
From blue water to a sad state of mind,
what meaning to "this" dream might I find?
Reality: The ringing of the telephone awakens me.
Leave me be!
The memory of the dream lingers.
Oh the subconscious mind in its dream state...
I'm so tired...

Nancy L. Cox
Denver, CO

What John 3:16 Personally Means to Me

For God so loved the world that He gave His one and
and only Son, that whoever believes in Him shall not
perish but have eternal life John 3:16 NIV.

God not only loved the whole world but He also
loved me personally. He was willing to give His
only begotten Son to Calvary's Cross to die for
all of my sins. When I first decided to follow
Jesus Christ at the age of nine, I trusted Him

and believed in Him. What took longer for me
to learn was: I would not be able to perish in
all of my of my sins. But I would gain my very
own eternal life in my beloved Lord and my

precious Savior Jesus Christ. Just because He
was able to pay my sins debts, by dying in my
place. When He cried out from the cross, "It is
finished!" I first knew that my eternal life and

my everlasting salvation was secure. For when
I enter into His kingdom of Heaven, I know He is
watching and waiting for me to finally arrive
there. Because he really cares about me.

Roxanne Dubarry
Everett, WA

Apologize

What type of society
do we live in that
it's okay to make fun
of others, then to not
apologize?
Worse yet, don't acknowledge it
and not expect an apology
or have others apologize for
what they have said.

Jamie Fernandez
Victorville, CA

What Is Home?

It's a shelter, some say,
A place to go at night
After working all day.

The body rests, it's true,
But home comforts the mind,
And the soul's at peace, too.

Peace with self and with God
Transcends a circumstance,
A 'home' we all should trod.

Sheree S. Cobbs
Denham Springs, LA

Hope

Through cloddy ground, through a boulder's fissure,
A seed finds root in some dark enclosure
Just like Hope appearing in quietude
Unfolding dewy petals, moon-pale-hued,
Tinting the winding way with light enough
For a soul to journey in the questing.
And as the way seems long and grated rough,
Calming Hope crayons hushed places beside
Garden ponds with still waters mirroring
Serene, clear skies: the soul is fortified
For the pursuit with its necessary
Struggle, claiming all that it must carry.
Anyone flushed with Hope's moonlit glow knows
Another Hand has planted now Hope's Rose.

Carmen Marie Ruestow
Boulder, CO

Mystic Warrior What a Fascinating Scene

Dancing, swirling to the Native American music
Music that speaks of tribal customs and wars
Music, we don't understand that speaks of
Lost secrets and age-old ways
Primordial: composed when the earth was young

The dancer, a warrior, such an authentic costume
The dancer, handsome, savage, lean and muscular
Long black hair, swirling with his movements
Dancing, dancing to the music of the ancients

Trying to take a picture, trying to capture a moment
of this incredible scene
He looks at me, my camera, shakes his head no
I put my camera down disappointed

Watching this beautiful dancer, forceful
graceful as if he invented this dance
The other dancers following
mimicking his steps

The warrior is gone, only air where he danced
The other dancers still faithfully performing
The pictures I had taken only show them
Where, where is the mystic warrior?

Marcy L. Bowser
Newark, OH

The Loss of My Son (from a Grieving Mother)

I lay my head down
I cannot sleep
The pain and grief are just too deep
I busy myself by watching TV
And just for a moment my mind is set free

The movie ends and I sit and cry
And panic sets in and I ask God "Why?"
Why is my son not here anymore
Why weren't my prayers answered
I fall to the floor

I'm broken—I'm changed
I'm weak and feel old
While my son is walking on streets of gold
In Jesus' care and company
Does my beloved child ever think of me?

Not one day will pass that my heart will be whole
For the pain of my loss has taken its toll
I want to live life—but it's so hard to do
Knowing my son isn't here
Makes it hard to get through

Heaven bound when my time is done
Reunited with my son

Tracey Travis Lee
Landenberg, PA

There are no words. I lost my son John on August 1, 2023. That was the hardest moment of my life. I continue to grieve; however, I still have a lot to live for. Life will never be the same. This poem just flowed out of me one night after I lay my head down and had just got done watching TV. I know there are other mothers and fathers in my shoes and I am so sorry for your loss. My faith in Jesus is the only way I am getting through. God bless all of you.

My Friend

What is the making of a very good friend?
Not just in the beginning, but to the very end.
A friend is **forgiving** for the stupid things you say,
To understand the meaning and move on to another day.
A friend is **reliable** and be there when in need
To help you during difficult times, even take the lead.
A friend is **insightful** and understands the real you,
To give you good advice, in everything you do.
A friend is **encouraging** especially when you're down,
To cheer you up or make you laugh and always be around.
A friend is **nice**, someone with an upbeat positive feel,
To give a hug, or a friendly smile, just to keep it real.
A friend is **dependable**, when the unknown is in the air,
To do whatever is necessary, because they really do care.
I'm such a lucky person to have you close and by my side,
To help me enjoy each moment and be there for the ride.

Ed Kielkucki
Bethel, CT

Throughout my lifetime I have been fortunate to have made so many good friends. To each and every one of you, "thank you," for the inspiration of this poem. Good friends are hard to find. Love you all.

To Embrace Gratitude in Darkest Moments

The heavy misted dangerous cloak of COVID-19
Plunged our family into an exhaustive delay 7-2020
Our dear Marly's (Dad's) ashes forced to stay in CA
Gratitude, as we clung to patience in a very long wait
That miraculously COVID-19 became a lesser threat 2022
That handsome son-in-law Tom, our designated driver
Covered thousands of miles, everything seemed fine
Till we got to Iowa, drowned in nostalgia's time
Realism set in, our darkest moments were foreseen
Restrained, courageous, unfaltering steps, that's how
Lovely daughter Teresa carried Dad's ashes away
Gratitude, a gregarious time spent, family's warmth
And to reminiscence awhile on the Koth's Iowa farm
Fun 4th saw niece Becky, Dave, dogs stroked by Tom
Good sport Tom pampered till their naptime
Covered thousands of miles, everything seemed fine
Till we got to Four Corners, I was on fire, COVID-19
Previously, the kids had kept me from a dangerous fall
When fun turned into darkest moments we stood tall
Excruciating pain, I ended up in the ER on a bang 7-4-2023
Visitation came, concern, kids were very late
Teresa had made a prolonged stop to check out my home
A flickering light, a buzzing sound drove Tom
To the appliances and found burnt and melted wires
My two heroes saved my home from a devastating fire
In darkest moments, the Holy Spirit was always there

Ada E. Koth
Gilroy, CA

Since 7/4/2023, I've now been through almost everything imaginable. I have experienced many painful mental, physical life-threatening, darkened moments in my life. My veil of privacy is lifted. On July 4, 2023 my body shut down—pain worse than child birth—on morphine—required to wear a device—homebound remainder of my life. Without daughter, Teresa, son-in-law, Tom, I would be homeless in a crowded, lonely nursing home. Instead, a nurse comes into my home twice a week. I am surrounded by sunshine, especially Teresa, and my nurse. Oh lucky me!

Birds a Flirt'n

While out walking, an amazing thing I chanced to see.
Two frisky mockingbirds were a flirt'n in a tree.
They continued their flirt'n as they began to fly.
They swooped down low, and they fluttered up high.

They kept right on a flirt'n as they went for a walk.
Till they stopped their strutt'n for a little bird talk.
It was a little chirp, chirp and then a little chitchat.
It tickled my funny bone as I watched all that.

Next, they faced each other in a dance routine.
They sashayed with a rhythm that was smooth and clean.
She moved to the left, and he did, too.
Then they repeated to the right in an old soft shoe.

When they saw me a'gawking, they darted in some brush.
I guess they wanted their flirt'n to be kept hush hush.
It seemed they were saying, "This is just for us.
So, mind your own business, you old cuss."

You may not believe me, but this is all very true.
I feel so lucky to have seen it. I bet you would, too!

Rose Dyess Anderson
Ellisville, MS

My house is located on nine acres of land. Two of the acres are wooded areas. I also have trees on the seven acres that I keep mowed. My husband passed two years ago. Much of my time is spent alone. Walking my land and observing plants and animals, fills a good amount of my time. The occasion of the flirting birds happened as I was walking to my mailbox. In all my eighty-two years of life I had never seen birds dancing.

A Diamond in the Rough

In all life there will be ups and downs,
maybe feel like we are level to the ground.
Living in the rough, life can get tough.
If we put our faith and trust in God,
He will get us out of this mess;
it's only a test.
Pray that His little light shines like a diamond in the rough
and breaks the chain inside.
Polish it with His spirit to shine like pure gold
and to become whole in the midnight hour.
God will turn it around.
No more rough nights or days—take time to pray to the Father;
the future looks bright and the rough stands still for now.
To be in the rough can make you stronger and have a story to tell.
While living in the rough, God puts diamonds in our life.
Swept the rough under our feet!
Now we can tell the story to everyone we meet.

Joan Carter
Adairsville, GA

Love Chorus

O love of God how strong and true
Eternal and yet ever new
Uncomprehended and unbought
Beyond all knowledge and all thought
Blessed assurance Jesus is mine
O what a foretaste of glory divine
Heir of salvation purchase of God
Born of his spirit washed in His blood
Redeemed how I love to proclaim it
Redeemed by the love of the Lamb
Redeemed through His infinite mercy
His child and forever I am
One day He is coming back
What glory that will be
Wonderful is His love to me

Bernice Hooks
Chicago, IL

*Since Jesus first came to this earth, generations have been expecting His return. My
mother believed Jesus would return in her youth. Jesus said there would be wars
and rumors of war and distress of nations. When men say "peace, peace" then
comes sudden destruction. During the pandemic I lost loved ones, and recently
my closest sibling. Singing the good news of the gospel revives my spirit and I am
comforted. Jesus promised to come back after the gospel of the kingdom has gone
to the entire world. All in the graves will hear God's voice. Every eye will see Him
coming in the clouds with power and great glory. Halelujah!*

Faded Flower

How beautiful is your creation Lord
The flowers that cover the meadows
They spring forth, full of life
We are so blessed to have them
They were meant to bloom forever
Then in came the destroyer
Reaking havoc in his path
Causing the flowers to fade away
I'm like those fading flowers
I was called forth and brought to life
As all people are beautiful
The crown of God's creation
But as the fading flowers
The destroyer has reaked havoc
And caused me to age
My youth is fading away
But like the flowers in the spring
I will be renewed and live forever
I will be called forth by name
Me, a faded flower, will bloom again
In the new heaven and the new earth

Linda J. Knudsen
North Mankato, MN

In Oneness We Stand

There stands a wall of stones.
In each one I see its uniqueness.
Some perfect, some very rough,
each laid from the hands of life.
While some sparkle in the sunlight,
others crumble from the weight they carry.
Each weathering the elements,
holding their structure.
Like the bones of the body
amass together for a common
purpose, they create a oneness.
Separating and dividing space,
offering the illusion of boundaries and protection.
Holding their position only until
the day they begin to fall.

Sandra A. Young
Seneca Rocks, WV

Because I Do

"You need to stop reading books and do some work,"
my father would say, pointing his finger at me.
"There are always all kinds of jobs to be done
on a farm," he continued, then walked out.

"But, Dad…" I rarely got to finish what
I wanted to tell him. So, I would go do
a chore, which seemed to never end, while
thinking about a story rolling inside my head.

I wanted to tell him that the books,
stories, places, reached out to me,
went inside my body and thoughts.
The words and characters brought me
adventures I could only imagine.

Once, Dad asked me, "Why do you read so much?
Your nose is always in a book!" "Because I do!"
I replied. He shook his head then walked away.
I wanted him to understand. "I have a few more pages."

I swallowed back the lump in my throat,
"Because I do," I whispered, as tears formed.
With watering eyes, I closed the book, then followed him.
I loved him so much. I was twelve. He did not understand.

Ronald M. Ruble
Huron, OH

There Was a Time

There was a time you made me feel like no other.
You reached out and hugged my heart.
An enveloping all warm sensation
like nothing I have ever felt.
There was a time
I believed your eyes.
I believed your heart.
I believed your touch.
An incomprehensible but punctuated
moment of time.
A passionate experience I could never find.
You shattered walls with just your words.
Now forced to find solace in my lonely world.
There was a time
I believed your eyes.
I believed your heart.
I believed your touch.

Hawk Prime
Vergennes, VT

God Desired a Genesis of Man

God desired a being that looked like Him—human.
So He formed man from the clay of the earth, a masterpiece.
A proclaim wonderment and illusion, glowing in His image a
marvel to behold Man at last.
He shone lifeless without the will to move, just wet earth without
the ability to move, to talk, to touch, to smell, to wonder, to gaze,
to imagine,
to want to walk. Man in view, no life, no love, no brain, no capacity, just an
image a most splendid feature to behold. The God who made Heaven and
Earth the most high one, the Alpha and Omega, looked at him and desired
to see him move, his hands, his feet, his face, his body.
Then God blew into his nostrils stooping low towards him, and he catch
the fire of life into mans being. Then man opened his eyes and saw his
Aba, Father new, and most special full of love and grace with unending
favor slowly then he moved his face as all around him to view the
beautiful scenes of Earth the most beautiful garden scene ever, then
he zoomed into movement laughing and breathing in confidence and
self esteem so magnified by the most high Master Builder. Man at last
fresh from the wet earth, perfect human pleasing God before the fall.
Perfect human Adam.

Cynthia P. Grant
Tamarac, FL

*I am seventy-seven years of age and vibrant and young as ever. The Lord gives
me the strength I need. I have been writing poems ever since high school. I enjoy
writing imaginative. I am a grandmother and a great-grandmother from four
sons God gave me. They are all about their lives with different skills and talents.
My prayers are with them for the best they will offer this world through the most
high God. Thank you for this opportunity.*

Everlasting Presence

You live in my heart. I cannot deny Your presence.
Through the storms and all my fears
I am enlightened through Your love.
When my body had no strength
Your spirit lifts me up in grace.
How grateful I am for Your mercy every awakening day.
The many nights my pillow swallowed my every tear,
I knew it was You who washed my heartache away.
For many years I felt the never-ending winds of mental torment.
Thank you, Jesus, for salvation.
Glory to God as the Word of the Holy Scriptures
Began the transformation of the renewal of my mind.
A freedom that can only come through my Savior Jesus Christ!
Setting my mind free.
A new life, a new breath, a new journey.
My new life began in my elder years.
A new revelation was birth as I learned that in Christ there were no
barriers— only eternal love.
Never forgetting the day of my salvation.
As a mere human I cannot deny I began to lose my life.
For no one comprehended my fears and my dismay.
My children, husband, my parents and all I love more than myself
Were unable to fill the death I was experiencing each day.
Every breath seemed to be my last as I gasped on my bed not knowing my
end.
I could barely lift my hands up as I looked up with no voice,
I cried in the lowest whisper, "Jesus where are You? Didn't You die for me?"
Instantly a realm of pure quietness and peace fell upon my being.
The relief was unbelievably unreal but undeniable in His presence.
I was saved in His embrace and everlasting presence!
Forever in Christ He made me His captive! Hallelujah!

Ipolita Sanchez
Brooklyn, NY

Another Time, Another Journey

Another time, another journey's end,
My final cry echoes within my mind.
My last words whispered to family and friends,
Until the next meeting, our fates entwined.

This seat, my throne, where thoughts collide,
Homicidal whispers fade away.
Negativity, a ghost of the past, I bide,
Life's speed, how did I get here, this very day?

Others' perceptions, deep within reside,
Life's twists and turns, a karmic play.
What goes around, they won't foresee,
Pain and sorrow followed me, a burning fray.

Good to bad, a transformation, instant and swift,
Anger fuels me, negativity my fray,
Day by day, I care less, my spirits lift,
Iced heart, I turn the other way.

Closer to perfection, as you get to know me,
In the final chapter, I cease this masquerade,
The past, the present, a tapestry, you'll see,
Wild thoughts conceived, nothing left, this path I've laid.

Emptiness, cruelty, a lone savage's creed,
The final destination, the journey's end,
Peace descends, my spirit is finally freed,
I am at home at last, where life and death blend.

Dalston Harrison Jr.
Brooklyn, NY

The World

The world that
I see is falling apart
with crisis
of anger flame
filled the air with
a crime of
scenery hate
words have no
forms are falling
from the lips
to witness the
senseless of act
remain in silent
through a broken
heart and a
despair soul
to confide the untold story
build with a shattered dream
of an urgent need from the tragedy
with an awakening call
remind us of the innocent loss
peace needs to take place
to define justice
to stop the chaos of all
for harmony to be maintained in unity

Hanh N. Chau
San Jose, CA

My Snow Globe

Snow-capped dreams
dominate my landscape,
becoming my new roads,
forming my new words.

Commitments to keep,
as I tread through squalls of indecision,
sometimes, driven only by instinct,
while trees hover over me as a marker of passage.

If only,
dreams were more expansive,
with less time devoted to departure,
I sigh.

If only,
blue skies could be kept inside lined pockets,
warming hands and warming hearts on icy shadows,
I cry.

All the while,
my inspiration remains,
remembering shivering on cold sleds as a child,
smiling at danger on that treacherous adventure,
dreaming downhill to Heaven.

Janet Margaret Grabarits Sforza
Northampton, PA

Making My Human Case

(In loving memory of my boyfriend LTC Carlos Best)

If I had wings that could highly soar
I would fly right up to Heaven
And I would open that door
I would ask God to let you come back
So we can love you some more

My tears would flow down my face
Way beyond measure I would tell God
That this one hurts so very much
Because you were an earthly treasure
To all of us

I would beg God so hard to allow
You to stay that my tremendous emotional
Distress would literally cause God's throne
In Heaven to vigorously shake

Even if God were to tell me NO!
He has the last word and final say
It would still be worth making
My point of view in my human case

LaTonya A. Seabrooks
Sacramento, CA

My poem was inspired by my boyfriend's death. I hope that I can bring some comfort to someone else and I hope this poem can also reach everyone who's ever lost someone whom they really loved and miss very much. This poem is dedicated to my boyfriend LTC Carlos Best family and friends. May this poem bless everybody's broken heart.

God Told Me a Secret!

The world we know is more of a shadow and an illusion,
A theatre that projects a hologram of mortal fancy.
Deriving its substance from an eternal, yet unseen reality.
It is transitory, finite, and incomplete, yet it can be renewed, remade, and
reprogrammed.
Within it a battle for our very souls!
It has one truth and one creator...with many counterfeits.
"For God so loved the world that He gave His only Son, so that everyone
who believes in Him might not perish but might have eternal life.
In its current state, it is passing away and will take all those who cling to it,
with it.
Be not anxious for the things of this world but seek God's Kingdom
beyond.
To believe is to be truly wise; it costs you nothing and may win you
everything...there is still time!

John Zarbo
Painesville, OH

I've always considered myself somewhat of an explorer. I love putting things together and noticing the extraordinary in the ordinary. Things are far deeper than we can imagine and at the same time as simple as can be. To be alive is to change the world or at least open its eyes. I have found that there are no accidents. We were known before the creation of the world and we are right where we are meant to be...and nothing can change that.

Haiku

serendipity
a propensity for life
singing and dancing

Beverly Mae Livernoche
Hampton Bays, NY

It is my pleasure to lead our Poets Rising group since 2011 at our local library monthly on a volunteer basis, meeting and greeting those, who for some, have come since the first meeting. It is a place where friendships are made. Poems, prose, anything goes...our motto. My thanks to those who help me continue this group and as of this writing, our future is solid, with God's help. Thank you all.

December Welcome

Alpine snow
Shimmering ribbon of light
Dances through the frosty blue
Stripes of indigo forest
Ripple over the mountains
Warm golden balls
Dot the glassy mirror
Icy lake gleams with
Cold glints of moonlight
Quiet slumbering town
Reflected in the winter twilight

Cynthia Powers
Statesville, NC

America

I woke up this morning
Jesus is in my heart.
Thank you Jesus
for doing Your part.

I believe the left
have gone crazy.
They have forgotten
we some day push daisy!

We all know the book
Held in God's hand.
With sorrow: I know
He looks down at His land!

Martha Kephart
Albuquerque, NM

Bottle of Love

As I reach for the bottle of love, as I open the bottle a beautiful smell of your perfume fills the air like an angel covering me with her wings. As I put the bottle of love to my lips, as I take a sip from the bottle of love I can taste your lips of cherry lip gloss as I take another drink from the bottle of love and feeling drunk on your love'n. As the bottle of love kisses my lips with your lips as I see your eyes looking into mine is like music to my ears. Such a beautiful day to be drunk on your love'n forever and always.

Don James Spence
Akron, OH

The "Bottle of Love" is my ideal of how love should be. I myself have been alone for sixteen years now, plus am recovering from open heart surgery. Life has been crazy for me. As I keep pushing forward hoping one day I won't be alone ever again. My name is Don Spence and I have been writing poetry on and off for twenty years. I have ten different poems published in books around the world.

What Is a Mom?

She is the person who
knew us and loved us
before we were born.

She cradled and held us
after nightmares and scary storms.

She lends an ear
when we need to talk,
sometimes about nothing,
other times about a lot.

She offers her shoulder
to lean on, followed by a hug so secure.
Letting us know,
we are safe in a crumbling world.

What is a mom?
She's so much more!

She's a blessing, a gift
A relationship that will never end.
Even when we as children are adults, no longer kids.

Julie K. Brincks
Johnson, KS

For You, I Came!

I left My glory
And came down to Earth
In a lowly way
Of a child's birth.

I grew through the years,
Overcoming all temptation,
So I could present Myself,
A sacrifice for your salvation.

Throughout My ministry,
I did My Father's will,
Even knowing that one day,
For sin, My blood would spill.

I suffered the cross;
Loving you kept Me there
Because I wanted a
Relationship we could share.

Dying for you so I
Could wash away your sin.
And once you've asked,
I'll come live within!

It is for you I came
And all others, too!
Because I want to spend
Eternity with you!

Neal A. Carl
Endicott, NY

Sad Lady

I see her each morning when she passes my way,
her shoulders drawn, her eyes dark with sadness,
no sparkle to brighten her day.
She never said a word; nor did I.
She seemed so sad. I wondered why?
I looked for her each day, though didn't know why.
Could I help her through her sadness, I wondered; I sighed.
Words never came. I looked; I stared.
Going our separate way, same thing every day.
One day she didn't pass; fear flooded my heart.
I should have said something, help her get a fresh start.
Didn't know her name; never saw her again.
But I miss her as if I'd lost my best friend.
I've learned to be friends to all, help each other stand tall.
I'll always remember the lady drawn and sad;
she will always be with me through the good and the bad.
Never forget to lend a hand; that's what they're for!

Thomas Dutcher
Myrtle Beach, SC

At Oakland Mill

Strolling along at the old Oakland mill
Suddenly he paused and stood dead still.
Standing by an old wall of dry stone,
He felt at home and not at all alone.

Feeling the warmth of loved ones dear,
Time folded back and they felt so near.
Hugs and kisses, long lost, back again.
He wanted to weep, but he had to grin.

Happy day visions swept over that hill.
Spurred by the blades of that old mill.
And as the miller packed the flour he'd made,
My friend had to go, but he wished he'd stayed.

Looks of peace crossed over that man's face.
He'd transended to another time and place.
He'd walked with spirits on that magical day,
There's no doubt about it! That's all one can say.

Tina Stoneking-Trujillo
Taos, NM

Martyr

I see the signs of the times
See truth turned to fiction
Struggling to survive
To exist, to breathe free
Surrounded by robots
Automatic soulless responses
Lock step with lies and deception
Alone walking in God's truth
Knowing to speak out
To shut down the lies
Will lead to eradication
My life before the judgment seat
Tried before men
I speak the truth
Amid a roar of lies
And spears of hate
Crucify *Him!*
Crucify Him!
C R U C I F Y H I M!
My arms outstretched
Embrace the world
That murdered me
   Truth

Paula Compo-Pratt
Westville, NJ

God's Word Is Truth

He lives in a barn and believes he's a cow
A man thinks he is Napolean, is it plain to you now
What do they have in common—can you understand and see
They live in another world called unreality.

Unreality means something is not true
You can "say" you are a cow; but really, are you?
To know what truth is and right from wrong
It all comes from the Bible; it keeps you strong.

The truth is "man and woman created He them."
There is good, there is evil, and evil is sin.
Little children and teenagers too
God created perfection and that was you.

Don't destroy what you truly are, a gift of love.
Your DNA, your body parts God sent down from above.
There will never be another just like you
So accept your birth body and believe that it's true.

It will save you years of heartache and pain
Mental anxiety and mental insane.
Follow after righteousness, believe His Word is true;
You will have a normal life and peace will come to you.

Shalom Christina Zoë
Roswell, NM

I wrote this poem because I see all the heartache of the children! I wanted to prevent their pain if I could. When a person rejects the truth, no matter what it is, all that is left is a lie. If they believe the lie, that opens the door for evil spirits to harrass and torment their mind. The world doesn't know how to fight that. 2 Corinthians 10:4-6 My book called Purple Eyes *is on Amazon, Barnes and Noble. But to see it, you also have to add my name, Shalom.*

A New Creation

Christian doctrine told me of my original sin.
Tainted by my birth, I am a sinner.
Satan thought he had me in the grave,
As each day the son rose up and the son set.
Life filled with good times and bad times,
I wondered how much time I had,
To love—to be loved.
What would I do with my time?
I wondered if Hell was my destiny?
Jesus said, "Not just yet."
I read the Bible about me and God's amazing grace.
Now people say that I am not the person I was.
I've been washed in the holy water of baptism.
I've been bought by the blood of Jesus.
By faith I'm a child of God—
A sinner—Born again—resurrected—forgiven.
That's who I am for all eternity.
A new creation!

Bill M. Watt
Junction City, KS

Breathe

Breathe—
Work little heart;
I do not want to leave
Or suddenly depart.

I have a million things to do
And they are here—
Not in the far and distant blue
Too many trials to bear.

Give me strength and peace;
Let me gain a way
To learn to slow my pace
To fulfill the goals I may.

Bring the force into my life
To strengthen my resolve—
Help rid this world of strife
To grow and to evolve.

Just breathe ---

Judith Parrish Broadbent
Chapel Hill, TN

Living in the modern world is a real challenge and age does not help. Working for peace and understanding is only something one person can do at a time.

Why Love?

Why must we love? Love is for fools, only a game, a game with no rules
A game with no rules, a game with no end, why do we play this game full
of chances we may never win?
We are nothing without love, or so they say. Hah!
We are nothing at all...merely pieces of clay...
Clay! Clay to be molded by rough hands and cold hearts
clay to be played with soon crumbled and tossed
So what? What is love? Is love not like the clay? Only an element just
a vague form...
Soon to be scattered then ultimately lost, forever forgotten
Are we not a substance?
Yes only a substance from Earth once wrought...
Are we not remolded again and again?
If we are only a substance from earth to remain
What then is love? Why do we play? Only a game.

Cenne Lynn Ryan
Miami, AZ

The Journey

I would rise like a star in the sky
The wind whispered and would breathe new light in me
Seagulls would glide with the sun and the fog
As I stood on the long, lonely shore

The sea meant everything to me
It captured the freedom in me
Walking on a village in a nearby town
Is like walking through the Journey of the Magi

My life is like the shadows that I wrote a year ago
But my heart is much clearer
because I'm letting in the rain
Time touches everything that 'The Window' could not see
It's even touching a light in me

The cold wind continues on this long, lonely shore
Timeless moments follow the sea
My new heart belongs here, in the breath of the wind
A birth in an older man

Gilbert Reynosa
La Verne, CA

To my beloved mother

My Promises—God's Gifts

Gifts a promise of life

I give promises to you
   You give life's gifts to me
I send my messages to you in prayer
   You send me the gift of life and living
I send you prayers of hopes and needs
   You send me the gift of fulfillment
I send you a thought of thanks for this day
   You send me sunshine and blue skies
I send you my daily prayers
   You send me this day to pray
I send you my book of life
   You send me the words that have been written
I send to you my love of being
   You send me your reason for being
I send to you my prayers for all
   You send to me the power of prayers

Always take time for solace in prayer
And give thanks for the strength sent to you.
Blessings from above are always all around us all.

Janet Toole
Tecumseh, MI

The Beautiful Mountains

Up in the mountains high in the hills
Late at night comes the sound
of the whip-poor-wills

The owl hoots with all of his might
When darkness comes and turns into night

During the daytime a cool
gentle breeze fills the air
The mountain beauty is everywhere

Mountain laurel trees are growing everywhere
Watered by the dew and rain there

The eagle soars so very high
Trying hard to touch the sky

The mountains are so beautiful
and beyond compare

As a gentle breeze fills the air
Yes, as a gentle breeze fills the air

Bobbi Jo Hager
Ozark, AL

Bridge above the Fog

A heavy fog has settled in the valley
Thick and dense
I cannot watch the hillside dwellers
Above the mist
Visibility is dismal
A sorry sight to see
Penetration impossible
In a perception impaired reality
Much too cloudy to navigate
Slumbering down, down
Down to the shores of the lake
Lethargic to the world
I must try to reach the bridge
Way up high, to see my girl
Soften the borders, the perimeters...
The edges of dreams
Truth is vaguely abstract
Not exactly what it seems
The bridge is much too fragile
Wooden steps, feebly weak
Just a few words
Are left to speak
The girl comes down from the mountain
To guide my way to the sky
But I cannot pay the price
Inflation's made it much too high

Jim Barker
Maricopa, CA

A Clear Horizon

We look for that clear horizon somewhere in time. It makes us think
    of summer roses with beauty entwined.
Maybe it's just over the next hill we must climb.
We think of simple things that can make our hearts be glad.
A clear horizon is not an easy thing to find with all life's problems
    it boggles the mind.
We should perhaps begin to grasp the things that make us happy.
Then that clear horizon we will find.

Epilogue
As we search for that clear horizon, we must keep one thing in mind
    and count the blessings bestowed on us by the Lord divine.

James Harwood
Spencer, WI

I was inspired to write this poem because of the trials each of us face in our daily lives. Sometimes we complain about what we don't have instead of counting the blessings that we do have. I visit the nursing home regularly and read poetry to those who enjoy it. Then I thank the Lord I can still walk in and out on my own. It was once said "I complained I had no shoes until I saw the man with no feet." I have six wonderful children and many grandchildren. My hobbies are poetry and vintage electronics.

Do You Love America? Then Vote Accordingly!

Our country has always been a democracy,
but some would change it into an autocracy!
I truly hope that this will never be,
and that we'll vote to remain a free country!

Since our economy is currently very strong,
and our businesses are moving right along,
there really is no reason to rock the boat,
so please think twice before you vote!

Of course, we must always do what's best,
for ourselves, and for all the rest.
So, please vote your heart as best as you can,
for if you do so, the future of America will be grand!

This upcoming election will be epic, that's for sure,
so please choose wisely so that our democracy endures.
Otherwise, we may likely regret how things turn out.
Of that I'm certain. In fact, I have absolutely no doubt!

Thomas S. Parish
Topeka, KS

As the election draws nearer and nearer, the republican party pushes more and more fear! Meanwhile, the democrats have sought to push changes without gloating, like passing progressive ways to deal with immigration and promote open voting. Curiously, under FDR the republicans were more inclined to simply say "Me, too," but now the Trumpers prefer to counter with objections to any proposed rule! Previously, republicans and democrats often worked out their differences, but now the republicans seem to simply want to make noisy appearances.

Bring on the Sunshine

As the day begins to break
We see the sun begin to shine
As his eyes begin to open
We see the face of God
Shining bright all around
As its rays begin to glow
We fill His love
All of these things happen
When the sun began to shine

Ronald Leroy Grayson
Fayetteville, NC

This is dedicated to all of those who, at a period in their lives, cannot see the sun due to death of a loved one or friend or a very serious illness there is no cure for, and finally all POWs from all wars. Also dedicated to my mother Ramona Grayson who passed on as well as my lovely wife Gloria.

A Little Owl's Prayer

Deep within the trees, among the birds and bees,
Lies a little baby hoot-owl, praying on its knees.

"Dear Father up above, provider of all love,
Look down upon this little bird, whose intellect is rough.

Your world has gone awry, when all's provided by and by,
Your humans fight and argue, though I really don't know why.

They grapple like the blackbirds, sequestering the food
And gang up on the rest of us residing in the wood.

Why can't humans be like owls, rejoicing in Your love
That everything that's needed is provided from above."

Douglas Allen Noel
Aiken, SC

In Between Two Worlds

In between two worlds
Not fitting in either one
Alone and lost sometimes
Suddenly I am found
Feeling the twilight of years
A generational era gone
Finding beauty in my age
Of a soul fine-tuned and honed
Was a long and winding road
Red flags, warning blinkers on
Extensions of my youth and fears
Laid to rest with headdress on
In the silences, I am alone
Listening to the sound of my heartbeat
Laughing at jokes I call my own
Sweet is the peace that invades me
As I paint what's floating inside me
Lost loves, lost lives, haunt me
Forever cherishing has been
Simplicity, synchronicity for a second
Is fleetingly gone again
Balance of circles revolving
Darkness at times, my friend
Walking in and out of light, again

Karen Northcutt-Miranda
Tucson, AZ

Age, to age with grace and beauty. Carrying forth the idea and creds of a past long list era.

Trust in the Lord

Trust in the Lord with all of your heart and He will direct your path,
Even when the road you walk, others mock and laugh.
Trust in the Lord for guidance as you humbly walk with Him,
Trust Him to keep the enemy away and from tempting you to sin.
Trust in the Lord with all of your heart and He shall help you see,
Which way to go, which path to choose, His light with you shall be.
Trust in the Lord with all of your heart and He will show you truth,
He'll brighten up the path you walk, with Him you'll never lose.
Trust in the Lord with all of your heart, He'll keep you safe and warm,
He'll comfort and protect His child, He'll keep you from all harm.
Trust in the Lord with all of your heart and He will show you love.
He'll give you many blessings as you trust in Him above.
The most important question that everyone should ask,
Is where will I spend eternity, when my life on earth has passed?
Will it be with God in Heaven with Jesus by His side,
In a world of love and perfection, truly a paradise?
Or will it be with the enemy in a world of demonic reign,
Enduring endless sufferings and constant torture and pain?
Ask the Lord Jesus to come in to your heart erasing all sin in your life,
He will forgive and walk with you as He promised you eternal life.
Trust in the Lord with all of your heart, when the enemy wants you to fall,
Just watch and see this enemy flee, when he sees the Almighty God of all!

Darlene Ware Horzepa
Ormond Beach, FL

Alzheimer's

I wonder what it's like to slowly lose your mind
You don't remember the time
Your clothes felt tight and weren't put on right
Life feels like it's passing you by
And when you look in the mirror you wonder if life is just one big lie
Your life is blown out like an old kerosene lamp
Like from the days of ol'
From the cold
Born young into a world of old
And gone like a thief in the night
No sound or worry in the world
Gone without a trace
Gone like the wind
As you brace yourself from the cold
And silently you let go
No place to call home
You look to the sky
You cannot deny
He is there
You must dare
To look beyond
For He will guide you out of despair
And into the light
You must plight
For His might
For He shall give you His sight.

Katie Chyma
Tama, IA

Last Flight of the Red Baron

With a spin of the propeller
The engine crackles and sputters
The pilot's uniform, stellar
The blood red Fokker triplane shudders
As it lurches forward and starts to roll
It leans into the sky and flutters
Baron Von Richthofen is airborne once more
He flies the triplane o'er the battlefield of France
Seeking a lone flier to increase his score
He stares into the clouds as if in a trance
Suddenly, a dark green British Sopwith Camel
Dives on the triplane from above, guns blazing
Richthofen shoves the stick forward
Pushing the triplane into a steep dive
Increasing speed and moving onward
Like bees fleeing from a burning hive
Bullets whiz by and tear into the red
Fabric covered fuselage of the plane
The British pilot maneuvers behind the ace
Firing short bursts into the back of the plane
The triplane barrel rows in a hurried pace
Rolling and twisting but it's all in vane
A speeding bullet strikes the Baron in the face
The burning triplane spirals downward in a spin
Crashing with a thud into the desolate plain
and the Red Baron will score no more

Harry C. Craft III
Wesley Chapel, FL

Such Memories

How fond the thoughts of yesterday
Reminiscence that do not stay
Sentimental of great times
hearts, flowers, and sunshine
Smiling and laughter we always yearned
From Granny's advice we could always learn
That memories are yours to keep and store
To love, cherish, and adore
But such memories feel free to keep
Because sometimes you will ponder and weep
Oh such memories

Gladine P. Bruer
Manvel, TX

Gladine Pannell Bruer is married to Carl L. Bruer, Sr., has three children Mike, Carl Jr., and Denitra, and seven grandchildren Carl 3rd, D'Andre, Avery, Tyler, Naomi, Caiden, and Carmela. She is originally from South Charleston, WV. Residing as of 2021 in Houston, TX. She is the author of the books Reflection from the Heart *and* Through the Eyes of My Joy *(poetry).*

What I'm Thinking Of

I'm thinking of the sun,
I'm thinking of the sky,
I think I want to live.
I'm thinking of the birds,
I'm thinking of the trees,
I'm thinking of wonder
And being pulled under.
I'm thinking of death,
And if I can task it.
I can't give up,
I can't give up now.
Thinking of the clouds,
I'm thinking of bread,
There's nothing instead.
I'm thinking of my past,
The devil might've won.
My body is torn
From thinking of a war.
I'm thinking of leaving,
Walking out the door.
I'm thinking of the end
When my mind will bend.
I'm thinking of staying,
When I want to run.

Maxwell P. Collier
Oakland, CA

Beloved from the Stars

From the unconditional love that glistens from above
Upon ethereal rays that beam across the sky
Within the solar plexus of the human eye
The epitome of a euphoric trance on the rise

Through the blood of mankind that radiates
An unseen rule of the Earth that aberrates

Beneath the cellular nervous system that lies beneath
From the air that circulates the essence we breathe

There is a transcendent glow from a perfect creator
Manifested from an elemental collision
Of an eccentric division

To be the very foundational form
Of what all living things are composed of
To have our very names written
Within the interior of collapsing stars

Thus, we are made so vibrantly
Out of the iridescence of star dust
That encapsulates the universe
Into one being

The very essence of love and life, in one breath

Bree Martinson
Gillette, WY

To Love God: to Love Others

A path to our Lord up above
A way of life showing to God all our love
To love our God and Lord supreme
Pray to God and be redeemed
To love all others around us
See to love our God and others a must
As God's spirit leads our way
In all we do in every way
God's grace and forgiveness covers us all
Our path and purpose as we are all called
To pray to our Savior is the key
To be blessed is to receive what we will need
So let God guide us in everything
And our love will show as our heart sings
God's blessing in abundance for everyone
This is the work of God and His work will be done
So draw close to God thru prayer
Showing desire to learn and care
We know the law tells us to love
Everyone and God above
So as we love God and all others
Grace for our sin God has us all covered

Michael Warren Hartl
Manheim, PA

Winter Joy

Oh how I love the winter;
I think that it's a blast,
But perhaps a week or two
Is all that it should last.

Sleet and snow don't bother me;
I find them both a treat.
But please not on the sidewalks,
Alleys, cars, or streets.

Snowflakes are so lovely
When on my glove they set;
Each one is quite special,
But why are they so wet?

I must say that this season
Is one that I adore;
Of all the seasons out there,
It ranks in my top four.

With holidays abundant
And their decorations bold,
Of course I love the winter;
I just wish it wasn't cold.

Linda Fusek
Chicago, IL

Gram I Am

I am old, said Gram I am.
My story is told,
Begins with a blam.
Never was I meant to be here now.
So let me munch this tasty cow.
Eat my bacon by the pound.
Walk with bare feet on the ground.
Don't make me put a helmet on.
Just let me fall out on the lawn.
Sunshine rain and
Bluey skies.
I'm still here,
I don't know whys.

Barbara Gulas-Wilson
Las Vegas, NV

I have enjoyed writing poetry for fifty years. At this point in my life, I am helping to raise my four-year-old grandson, Mason. He already knows how to read. This poem I wrote is in the style of Theodor Seuss Geisel, AKA Dr. Seuss. I would like to dedicate it to my grandson.

My Feet

Nothing you say or do
Will defeat
The way I feel
About my feet
I love the crooked slant
They have
And growing corn
Is not so bad
They have gotten me
All around
And when they're tired
I sit down
They let me know
If I've stood to long
They sing It hurts
Just like a song
And I don't know
What I would do
If I had no feet
To wear my shoes
So here's to you
My little doves
With all my heart, soul
And love
Together, forever
We will always be
And if you don't believe it
You just wait and see

Suzan Lewis-Escalona
Torrance, CA

Haiku

Those departed walk
with softer footfalls in paths
where we saw them last.

Robbie Tynes
Ardmore, OK

Daily Duties

I cook
I clean
I do all that
I trim his beard
I trim the fat
Off his steak
Every day
Though when I say
"I love you"
He is still filled with dismay
For no matter how many times I give him my all
No matter how many times I am at his beck and call
It is always a chore to love—
Me.

Shaila Quaintance
Orlando, FL

The Wizard of Was

I pulled back the curtain and what did I see!?
The obomination... staring back at me.

The old man with the wax face was being controlled:
All strings in place, all strings being pulled.
The "fundamental changes" now nearly complete:
The eagle almost gutted, trampled under his feet.

Weaken the military, take authority from police
Trouble the races, stir suspicion and grief.
Make the innocent the enemy, pervert justice and truth
Have the media lie and manipulate the news.

Until border-less and broken, overrun and complex
Thru gangs, Fentanyl poisoning and trafficking of sex,
The new Babylon rises and the coup is complete
The eagle just gave up the ghost...
And lies dead at his feet.

Rhonda S. Galizia
Zelienople, PA

If the watchman sees the sword coming but does not warn the people and the sword takes the life of one of them, that man will be taken in his sin, but I will hold the watchman accountable for his blood. Ezekiel 33:6-7 Revelation gifts operate in the watchman as the Lord wills. Through Holy Ghost discernment in prayer, fasting and meditation in the Word, a watchman receives words of knowledge and wisdom, and is given ability to discern the demonic power behind a situation/ person. Watchman is only responsible for giving the warning, not for how people react.

True Valentines

Oh for the Love
That rescued me
Before this world
Came to be

He who created all
Before the universe was
Felt within His heart
Love for one so small

Time came to be
When the universe began
The Passion for it to be
Was driven by His love for me

Each one of us
Our Creator knows us by name
He knew the price He had to pay
His blood shed in Love for me

Sharon Elaine Eoff
Moscow Mills, MO

This poem came to me while I was going through my emails for the day. Love, real love, is unconditional with no boundaries and no sacrifice too small or great. Our Creator loves us that much.

My Sweet Isabella

My favorite hello
My hardest goodbye
Not by my side
But forever in my heart and mind

Man's best friend?
Oh! No
My Bella Boo
You were so much more till the end

My family
My secret keeper
My troublemaker
My therapist, too

Four years were just too short
What I wouldn't give for just one more
You were the best mental health support
One day I'll meet you on the shore

I'll meet you at the end of the rainbow bridge.

Heather Sievert
Beaver Dam, WI

I'm just a heartbroken girl who misses her dog.

Keep Your Crown

Always keep on your crown
Remember, no matter what
You were meant to be a queen
Keep your head held high

Don't allow anyone to disrespect or demean
Who you are and meant to be
Always be true to you
Follow your passion, wherever it leads

It was placed in your heart long ago
To lead you to your true path, and calling
Only there will you find your purpose
Placed before you were born

Along the way, many enter your journey
Keep only those that help you grow
Don't let anyone take you off your path
If you get lost, pray for the way home

For your bridegroom awaits
Your presence as his queen
Always keep on your crown
For your groom is a king

Diane Basile
Goodyear, AZ

Tiger Dear

Where did you com from, Tiger dear?
From out of Heaven down to here.

What makes your eyes so bright and gold?
Reflections from Heaven's streets I'm told.

What makes your forehead so smooth and high?
An angel touched it as I went by.

Where did you get that warm purr of bliss?
Two angels at once gave me a kiss.

Where did you get that tail fur coat all?
It all came together in a little ball.

How did all these things become you?
God thought about me and so I grew.

How did you come to me my dear?
God thought about you, that's why I'm here!

Stephen Williams
Tulsa, OK

Return to God, America!

Return to the God of our fathers.
Stand boldly before His face.
Receive His love beyond measure,
Dispensed by His Holy Grace.

Nothing shall be impossible!
Take hold of His outstretched hand.
Just as is written in scripture,
He'll lead you to His promised land.

Hear, see and do what He's spoken
And that which He's speaking today.
Provision is signed, sealed and paid for
By Jesus, the life, truth and way.

Roberta M. Spinney
Eliot, ME

Did I

Did I leave you without saying goodbye
Did I leave you without kissing you and it made you cry
Did I not tell you how much I love you and how much you mean to me
Did I not tell you, you are my wife to be
Did I promise to be there for you through good and bad times
Did I not tell you I wanted you to be mine all mine
Did I fail to tell you how beautiful you are
Up close in person and from afar
Did I not tell you how much I love making love to your mind
And your body over and over again
And over, and over, and over again
Did I not tell you I cannot wait to see you and hold you in my arms
Did I not tell you I want to fill you with all of my charms
Because if I did, I meant from the bottom of my heart
Because if I did, we will always be together and will never part
I have conveyed a lot of things to you that are true
But most of all I love you
I love you a thousand times
And a thousand times I love you more

Raymond A. Thomas
Richmond, VA

Birthday Greeting

Your birthday is here
Time for cake, ice cream, and cheer
and gifts that will delight
Your special day to celebrate you!
Happy birthday and best wishes!

Dorothy Ann Harris Moy
Southfield, MI

Anxiety in Love

It's still hard to say,
How much you make my day.
Sometimes all that brings is worry.
What if the lines get blurry?
Maybe I will always be uncomfortable;
Eye contact is just too vulnerable.
You're so gentle and sweet;
Still I want to retreat.
How will the songs change,
As we turn another page?
I asked for a love like you.
Now what do I do?
I want to run away,
But hoping that you stay.

Willow Roberts
Virginia Beach, VA

What Will They Say?

They all have an opinion and need to
be heard, never to seek and find God's
word.

Lack of knowledge and wisdom fill the
air... lies, corruption, perversions they
bare.

Right is wrong...wrong is right
and laid out before us in plain sight.

Grace and mercy to those who repent;
the salvation message will never relent.

But, there does come a day when all
God's children are taken away.

Then, what will they say?

Marianne Ruth Gorman
Morrisonville, NY

My Present Life

I live in a singular world
for I am a senior citizen
The world is a large place
and serves a lot of people
Their needs are many and varied

I only want to be healthy
While I live here
I'll reach out to others
if they need to hear from me
as I've lived longer than some

I may have knowledge
and wisdom to share
and I'll be glad to do that
God expects me to do what I can

I do not know the future
or how much time belongs to me
I'll serve my Lord with my heart
as it pleases my Father.

Margaret Rahn
Yankton, SD

Narcissist/Opportunist

I thought I had met the "perfect man," at least he presented himself to be
a God-like man, portraying himself as a carbon copy of me! Now bear
in mind, we didn't meet face-to-face. This "new world order" of social
media dating, compounded and confused the matter at hand! For several
months, the talking and chatting was fine. We set goals, boundaries,
and clarified intentions, thus creating trust and respect. Then one day
a situation arose, he needed my help to guarantee its success! I thought
it was perfectly legit until I noticed the rest! I stood up, as only I can
do. Believing it was the company and their business tactics, I addressed
the matter at hand. As I withdrew my friendship he admitted he was
paying the price for his part in this manipulative plan! He begged for my
forgiveness and assured me he would settle the score; because I'm kind
and forgiving I gave him a second chance. What he didn't know and I
didn't reveal is that once burned, I don't forget the pain; until one day, my
spewing venom I returned! His words were: "I haven't had a Valentine's
Day gift since the passing of my late wife." I retorted: "You gold digger, live
with the memories of your past! Your narcissist ways have shown you the
door—get out of my life and return *no more!*"

Marlene Theressa Lewis
Brooklyn, NY

*I am an educator and I love writing poetry. I wrote this poem "Narcissist/
Opportunist" as a way of poking fun at social media dating but also as a means of
saying, be aware of the Narcissist personality disorder, who shows himself one way
but turns out to be only for himself.*

Express Yourself

So many ways you can express yourself
In creative writing, art, singing and dancing
So many expressive feelings in the heart
Let it out in the open; show who you really are inside and out

Have faith and believe in yourself; believe what's in your blood
Believe in what you want to do
I have faith in you

Have confidence in yourself
Encourage others you know and adore
Take this opportunity to find
Your wishes, your hopes, your dreams
And your passion will come true

To journey, to explore your opportunities
To be self confident
Be true and honest with yourself
Don't give up, keep trying until you got it

Express yourself in so many ways
Admire your adventures; your journey of opportunities
Think positive thoughts not negative
Trust me, I know what I am talking about
Its so hard but hang in there
It will show, you will shine

Danielle Elizabeth Barry
Myerstown, PA

Senior Discounts

No longer am I asked if I qualify for senior discounts.
When and how did this happen?
Aching joints, age spots, grey hair, and wrinkles...
The mirror clearly reflects 76 years of living.
In Australia I am the age of wisdom;
In America I am chronologically gifted.
I embrace this journey; I never have to be 20 again.
The realities of limitations are frustrating:
Three miles at high speed on the treadmill
Morphed into two at a moderate rate.
Treks on the mountain bike no longer feasible.
Depleted energy, sleepless nights...
This is retirement: a simpler life,
A good season.

Susan A. Cooper
Bryant Pond, ME

The author of Painful Passage, Joyful Journey, The Story of God and Me, *(published by Wipf-Stock, available on Amazon, ChristianBooks.com,...), poetry has been a mode of expression throughout my life. A retired professor of literature for children, adolescents, and young adults, I continue to write. Susan A. Cooper, EdD.*

Depend on Jesus

A life consists of dependency
It all begins at birth
Even though you didn't know
It began when you came to Earth
It eases in some ways as you grow
And increases in others though it might not show
And until you die no matter how great you are
You depend on someone or something
We feel independent when we go to work
And pay our share of life's many fees
It feels very nice to know that it is
Yourself who furnishes your needs
Don't push out your chest too far my dear
For realization will stop you dead
When you face a big problem you didn't expect
And you find that you need someone
You are not independent yet
Money is important to the rich and the poor
But money does not open every door
It seems to open them all if you don't care
About anything else and never share
But a door made of wood, metal or stone
And all the money you can hold
Cannot close the door of death
Or bring joyous relief to a hell-bent soul
Depend on Jesus

Carrie E. Bridges
Huntsville, AL

A Winter Tapestry

Tree branches bow low
Under a soft, white blanket
Of winter's first snow.

Stark branches stretch high
Framing the golden, bronze glow
Of a winter dawn's sky.

Falling light snowflakes
Dance to winter's slow rhythm
On deep, frozen lakes.

Winter's full-moon glow
Cast dancing shadows on ponds
Nature's half-time show.

Winter trees all bare
In a forest deep in snow
Sits the wary hare.

Weeping, melting snow
Clings to high, rocky ledges
As swollen brooks flow.

Stan A. Mendrick
Branchburg, NJ

Reality Is Bittersweet

Ghosts from the past haunt our souls
Mistakes revived
Smoke and mirrors; dreams and schemes
Truth and lies
Friends and lovers; parents and chldren
Hellos and goodbyes
Memories and flashbacks; gratitude and pleas
Prayers denied
Ups and downs; gains and losses
Goals retreat
Depressed or elated; quit and try again
Reality is bittersweet

Dianne Kaye Carter
Roseburg, OR

I write fiction suspense with the pen name Dianne Kaye and self-published Misled *in 2016,* Resolution *in 2020 and* Jaden's Grace *in 2024. Xlibris Publishing pitched the story as a cautionary tale of romance and a psychological thriller. While writing this trilogy, I was continually awestruck by the characters when they took on a life of their own. As soon as I gave them a name, some personality traits, and set them up in a scene with diaglogue, they came alive on the page. I summed up their trials and tribulations in* Jaden's Grace *with this poem.*

Pondering

I am a stow away
Have I always been?
So many fears
Are harbored within.

The destination is known
The course is clear
The ominous sea awaits
And I alone must steer.

Victory or defeat
Which awaits for me?
The revelation embarks
I must begin to be.

Shoreline sighted
Sails set
Wind is steady
Onward? Not yet!

Fears becalm me
And again I wait.
Ever drifting
Is that my fate?

Elissa Ann Murphy
Port Jefferson Station, NY

Sympathy Words

"I'm so sorry for your loss
and the inside pain you feel.
Your loved one has passed on,
leaving a hole in your family."

We write those words,
We believe those words,
But until it happens to us,
We can't really feel those words.

It's hard to lose someone you love.
I think they're watching from above,
Where there's no more sorrow or pain,
And the streets are washed with warm sweet rain.

They're now in a place of peace and joy,
In the holy presence of God's little boy.
They'll live on in your memory and heart
    where they'll always be a part
        of who you are.

Kris Schulz
White City, OR

Arrival

Feed me—feed me—feed me
The rain dispersed all night
Droplets still negotiating their complete downfall
Noting spring's arrival
The flowers were screaming with thirst
Feed me—feed me—feed me
I need to grow from the earth
To feel the luxury of living
Sprouting amazing hues of colors
Never a duplicate grows
Feed me—feed me—feed me
Perfuming the world with their individual fragrance
I want to live and feel the sun in the morning
With the early dew which helps me to grow
After the darkness escapes away
Feed me—feed me—feed me
It's my moment in life
I am here
Dressed magnificently
For my arrival
Feed me—feed me—feed me

Renata Dawidowicz
Madison Heights, MI

The Silence of Walls

If only the walls of old homes could speak
Of past residents' secrets, would they reveal
A secret room, rotten pipes that flow water or
Air.

Hidden gold or bones from terror or
Treasures beneath one's feet, like an empty
Cement pond.

If only the memories made from room to room
Year to year, decade to decade or beyond our history
Could speak of joy, sadness, wealth, or despair.

Would they say to a new prospective family,
Yes, I am fine, I need repair or I am dying.
Release my bounding walls and built a new.

If walls could only tell the secrets from the past would
They shed their knowledge to a prospective family or
Remain in silence.

Sharon L. Kasabian
Siloam Springs, AR

Untitled

The waves are crashing
 As I watch the ocean
This huge body of water
 Is filled with emotion
The tide is in The surf is high
 Reminds me of my moods
  So I turn and sigh

Shirley Harmison
Daytona Beach, FL

Babe Don't Go

Babe, don't go!
And leave me here all alone,
making me walk and move along
with my shadow.
Going back to the days we first
met. We sat, we talked, we drove,
we bar-hopped together.
So now I'm walking these roads
alone again.
Babe, don't go! Don't break my
heart now that we are apart.
Babe, don't go.

Lawrence D. Student
Cleveland, OH

My Melanin Brother

My chocolate stick
My hot cocoa
With a twist

My chocolate bar
My melanin brother

Your skin is dark
Warm, and eyes
that look into my soul

The mind of a genius
An attitude of a king
standing tall

I love and adore you
my Melanin Brother

Yvonne Walters
Waterbury, CT

Offbeat Improv

It felt like a drama club.
Determined young faces without pretense,
doing a loose adaptation of everyday people.
A chorus of high-pitched voices made
the characters come to life in mime.
Scrunching their noses as they sip
imaginary cups of strong coffee,
tasting the bitterness of life.
Then dutifully flipping open laptops,
with fingers flying over the keyboards
like they were playing piano,
and yet not knowing how to tie their
shoelaces right to walk the walk.
Someone started to play an air guitar,
while the rest of us did backup percussions
to the upbeat rhythm of our hectic world,
moving in the bike lanes to avoid heavy traffic.
We are drawn to the avenues hoping that
what we are looking for has not vanished.
A stellar performance today,
and as if on cue the sun was setting
as we join the stars out at night.

Yvonne Gannon
Kaneohe, HI

*Surrounded by creative people completes a circle of friends. Join them in a small
café that serves as a meeting place as you read my poem "Offbeat Improv," where
reality with a sense of humor steals the show.*

The Flight of the Penis

How many times can you enter a room
Strong and cocky with no conscience
Traveling from place to place intent on
Conquering and devouring and yet

It stands to reason that sometimes you
Stumble upon that which is not holy
Leaving behind heartache and broken
Promises in your wake

Joyce Yvonne Childrey
Snellville, GA

Do You Ever

Do you ever just scream and nothing comes out?
Do you ever speak your mind without a doubt?
Do you ever disappear when no one is noticing?
Do you ever hate things that keep you from focusing?
Do you ever get rid of regrets causing you to fall?
Do you ever say the hell with it all?
Do you ever feel a rush that becomes your enemy?
Do you ever question your purpose with misery?
Will you ever stop being afraid
And enjoy life before you fade?

Pearl Maldonado
Hondo, TX

Magic

Magical, powerful, attractive, divine
Prosperity, abundance, and wealth are mine.
Happiness, health, love, and peace
Live in my heart and are part of me.
I dance with the spirits that live in the trees.
I breathe in the wind and bathe in the seas.
I speak my intentions to the stars and the moon.
I smell all the flowers as soon as they bloom.
I live in the moment,
And the moment lives in me.
I have faith in the universe.
I'm where I should be.

Becca Lynn Grant
Beacon Falls, CT

Look and listen inside yourself. Find what you believe in; find what nurtures and nourishes your soul. Find what works for you. You are magic; use it to your advantage.

Emotional Mind

Full of emotions, my mind may say no
My heart might say yes
My dialog might express I am fine
My mind might scream otherwise
Just can't help but go crazy inside
With the depth of feeling so deeply
You end up losing control
Emotional mind can't be at peace from it
Robbing emotional mind of all the joy
The wise mind logical as ever
Emotional mind gullible as they come
Vulnerable as they are in a crisis
The crisis being of one's heart
Putting often one foot in front of other
Staying headstrong but time to time
Losing your way hanging on too much
There's always solutions behind confusion
And a smile for every tear
And a poet that shares her experiences of a year
With every rainstorm there's a rainbow
With every lie there's the truth
With every book there's a story
With every hardship there is wisdom
In every life a new path.

Alyssa Pascalli
College Point, NY

Poetic Justice

This summer
A spider's web
Was strung on my porch.
I swept it away,
And this fall
My house has gnats.

Richard Stepsay
Aurora, CO

Turning Ordinary

The dark slipped in so silently
I believed I was still sitting amidst the sun.
So when the rain reached my face it was cold,
reminding me of your past.
That I was not the first set of skin
you had ever laid your hands upon.
My eyes of cobalt were not the only pair
that you had drowned yourself in.
After the frigid shards of envisioning you
with another version of myself
finished cutting through my mind.
I was left feeling unattractively ordinary,
not special in the slightest.

Kristin Kane
Santa Barbara, CA

Let There Be Life #4

4:04 am November 17, 2023
The universe created the most handsome boy for us to see
Aloha! ArtLovian Clay Jones
The heavens blessed you with beautiful skin and strong bones
Today is the fourth day that our family lives on forever
Your brothers and sister will guide you through any weather
Sail the "water" and let Daddy and sister's "air" show you the "sign"
Your brothers and Mommy will open the "earth" for you to shine
You're our crust, mantle and core
The true elements that intertwined you to become our number four
You made it through the fall and didn't stumble into winter
Gearing up for the running season, long distance and future sprinter
Mommy was determined again, so we invested in your home birth
Daddy is thankful that we could never put a price on your worth
Like your father and eldest brother Artist, you were born on a Friday
Celebrating your life forever to part-tay!
Your birth was original as the topaz
Praying that your life forever will be smooth as jazz
"ArtLov" is "Our Love"
The sky has no limits precious dove
God said for the fourth time, "Let there be life"
Thanking your mother and our midwife
I wished upon a star and my dreams really came true
Proud to be a father of four, thanking God for you!

Artist Clay Jones
Fort Belvoir, VA

Hello again, Poetry Nation! This is my thirteenth published poem! This poem was inspired by the birth of my fourth child, ArtLovian Clay Jones! Having him here at home for our second consecutive home birth in two years was an amazing and incredible experience! His mother, LoveLeigh, two brothers, Artist II, Aquarian, sister, LoveLeiella and I, are so excited to finally have him here! My wife LoveLeigh delivered all four of our kids natural without any pain medication. She is a true champion and "I Love Her More Than Most!" God continues to bless our family and I'm truly thankful!

Closing Bell

I hear the bell,
Almost inviting,
As it peals for me
With peaceful tiding.

Years of tears
And tribulation,
Fertile fields
Of adulation.

Harvest left
For those who see
The earthly merits
And memories.

Hence the value
Of wise endurance
And not forgetting
The heavenly insurance.

Camille Einoder
Homosassa, FL

Forest Dream

With a flurry of activity in the forest of a dream
Comes the realization of a glowing light beam.

Escorted to a place unknown, but familiar it would seem
Surrounded by a somewhat serious, organized team.

A bubble of fluffy clear light contained
Only an uncertain knowledge of my presence remained.

Time shifting dimension quietly set in place
Uneasy and unsure, but comfortable in space.

Unceremonious dismissal apparently occurred
Left with more knowledge, yet all methods blurred.

Too confused to understand or recognize faces
It seems light emerges from the darkest places.

Darryl Monteiro
Fall River, MA

Life

With the heart of a gambler
He studied the hand
Life had dealt him
This was a game
He knew how to play
No way could he lose
The joker just smiled
He understood the rules
The dealer takes all

Marlys Daerda
Renville, MN

Moments

Life started in a garden.
Love grew and changed the
meaning of being.
Shared moments, alone and quiet
moments, happy and sad moments
happen in life's garden.
Animals, birds, and insects
share the garden and the
protector and keeper of God's
garden is St. Francis.
Enjoy all the moments.

David Hayes
Woodland, CA

Golden Portrait of God

A mist, a turn into the Burgundy Balance of Bells!
Ringing joy it's call Heaven.
It's a star of diamond aglow. God's portrait is lovely.
God loves us so much. He will bring all to Heavens stairs,
Must be wise, and be brilliant, to find love in the silvery beams.
God's eyes of purity will give happiness, and all in His domain
will sparkle and behold radiance.
Bells are singing, and children playing a passion indeed.
Flowers are glowing, in the stormy wind, because Heaven is
flowing like the Great Danube River. And deep thought bind, to
golden poetry, is alive and growing in the honor of the sweet
mind of all men.
Poetry is music to God's heart and soul, miracles and blessings
welcome to all poets.
Poets highly praise and classified, as a ticket to the train
of Heaven.
Poetry is a beloved musical and melody for all mankind.

Catherine C. Inserra
Clifton, NJ

I was born on July, 1937, in Paterson, NJ. Had nine children, wrote book about Vigils of Religious Poems. Wrote songs and other poems. I feel happy when I write poetry. Went to Palmer's Writing School. Poetry makes you close to God. Poetry makes you happy. God bless everyone who loves poetry.

A Love Story

Not a day goes by,
I get a glimpse of you.
I can't stop smiling with love in my eyes.
Every time I wake up next to you,
I cherish the moment every morning.
I sneak back into your arms and stay there for awhile.

Not a night goes by,
I get touched by you.
As you put your arms around me,
you give me a simple kiss goodnight.
We stare at each other for awhile,
until we fall asleep and dream.

On our wedding day,
our everlasting vow of love begins.
Something was borrowed, something was old,
something was blue, and something was new.
My dad walks me down the aisle,
and we say our I do's and kiss.

Nine months later,
we welcome our twin babies
with open arms.
A boy and a girl were born.
A new beginning is coming ahead for both of us.

Laura M. Keifer
Amsterdam, NY

Arrival of Spring

Splashing in the rain
Making mudpies in the puddles
Yellow boots maintain
Fun in the ripples.

Sliding in the wet dew
And catching raindrops,
None of them too few,
Until the water completely stops.

Krisann Johnson
Richmond, IN

Tantrum

Stomp, stomp
Pout, pout
Whine, whine
Shout, shout
Whimper, whimper
Cry, cry
Hold my breath
Cover my eyes
Refuse to eat
Except for sweets
Now my tantrum is complete.

Suki R. Kaplan
Glastonbury, CT

The Darkness

Am I not in the land of my time
Where is peace
Where is family
Where is the friends

Why can't I feel happiness
I am in a place where loneliness
is closing in and my mind is
confused and wandering from place
to place I scream for love and
freedom from the darkness

I long for happiness to slip back in
and embrace me once again
I fear that time I once knew will
never return

The darkness I fear is here to stay
as it holds the world tight in its
grip hear my cry as I pray this
darkness will someday, somehow
meet its end and light will once
again embrace the world with love
and peace along with harmony

Barbara A. Kelley
Detroit, MI

Greetings to Mommy and Daddy

When Jesus said I was coming
I couldn't wait for us to meet,
Preparation began in Heaven
from my head to my feet.

I was fitted with two little eyes,
A little round nose,
Ten little fingers,
and ten little toes.

All the rest especially designed
by only God's command.
"So hello," you have a finished product
created by God's unchanging hands.

When I left Heaven, I told them I'd be back,
but didn't know exactly when.
Hold the gate wide open, and someday
I'll return with Mom and Dad, and lots of friends.

Brenda Richmond Gregory
Sevierville, TN

Splintered But Not Broken

My life feels like I have no purpose or hope.
I am seeking answers before the end of my rope.
Feelings seem splintered and shattered.
Wondering what really does matter.
I guess my heart is broken
by the hurtful words that were spoken.
I need to find joy in my heart again,
Looking for answers as to where to begin.
In my sadness and despair,
I am finding answers in my prayers.
The frown in my heart is keeping me down.
Now my answers have been found.
Once I listened and began to believe,
the Lord met me there and I began to receive.
I no longer feel weak, poor, and down.
Moreover, my heart is no longer bound.
My lack of hope is not what it seemed.
I feel joyful and I am redeemed.
The Lord met me in my strife.
In addition, He has given me a renewed life.
I was splintered but not broken,
Renewed by His precious words that were spoken.
I will continue to give my worries to the Lord
and look forward to His awesome reward.

Bonnie F. Tucker
Clarksburg, WV

America the ?

Remember Hitler
Idi Amin
Now there's Putin
And Xi Jinping

Putin just sits there smiling
Watching this country fall apart
Xi just sits there waiting
Observing the death of this nation's heart

Politics has become everything
With personal agendas and whims
No longer for the people
Freedoms, life, and liberties becoming dim

America is amassing enemies
At a breakneck speed
Willing to let the bad guys win
We are fast losing our lead

Losing the respect of those
Who once looked up to us
Watching our constitution
Being trampled into the dust

This is America
Where dictators have no place
Yet our courts and politicians concede
Anything—to win their ungodly race

Laura P. Smith
Pinebluff, NC

Homeless in America

Oh, we see them every day in stormy weather,
laying on a bus stop bench wrapped in a wet
blanket trying to stay warm from the cold wind.

Seasons seem harsh to those without the comfort
of the basic needs which you and I have in stormy
weather; we pass them by every day, yes! We are
obligated to stop and render help to the needy.

For whatever reason the homeless will always be
with us; their need is just like ours, the comfort
of shelter from stormy weather will never change.
We have the means to fill the emptiness they
experience daily in stormy weather; we must
brighten the life of just one person in need.

What will it take for America to change how
we view the needs of our brothers and sisters for
whatever reason are living in need of us.
We have the means to help just one person
in stormy weather.

Joe J. Espinoza
Glendale, AZ

Good Night, Sweet Dreams

good night sweet dreams
you beautiful child
I wish your dreams
are gentle and mild
of angels and puppies
of kittens who sneeze
Mickey mouse and Minnie
Miss Piggy with Kermit her devotees
of peppermint ice creams
rainbows and fairy queens
snowflakes with mittens
grandmas who are sitting
beside your pretty crib
and kissing your lip after lip
your soft and curly hair
protecting you in your layer
from COVID-19 and much more

Jutta Janotha-Woitscheck
Vero Beach, FL

Happiness Vs . . .

We search for happiness,
   It can be hard to find
Many go through troubles
   to find it's a state of mind.

Happiness from the outside
   Never seems to satisfy.
The longing from within
   That often passes us by.

Better is the need to search
   For something greater still.
It may go against all instincts
   Due to stubborness of the will.

A feeling so much greater,
   Which any evil cannot destroy,
Is reaching out to help another,
   That, my friend, is pure joy!

Michael Hamilton
Bourbonnais, IL

Love Shared

Love's not love till felt by two,
Only then may it be true.
For one who feels yet not felt for,
Feels the heartache nothing more.

But one whose love requited be,
Floats high above both land and sea.
Dreaming of a soft caress,
A touch of hands, a gentle kiss.

To be both loved and love another,
Ranks high above all man's endeavors.
For hearts enjoined forever be,
Now and for eternity.

Ken Frjelich
Deerfield, WI

Ms. Margaret

An angel with a dream softly approached God's throne
I'd like to have something to love of my very own
It's not that I don't love You Lord for You know I do
It's just that I believe I could love little humans, too
The Lord sighed deeply, then smiled as He said
I want to make sure you understand just what lies ahead
Becoming human with all their limitations and strife
You will also become a woman if your desire is to give life
Great physical pain escorts every child which you birth
As you begin your journey into motherhood on Earth
There is great joy and a love that you've never known
But more comes when raising little humans of your own
Sleepless nights endless days heartache beyond measure
Triumphs, love, hugs, and kisses you will treasure
In time you'll send them out on a journey of their own
Praying they remember the love and life lessons from home
I will grant you this request because you will succeed
For the cost of loving little humans is great indeed
When your time on Earth is done, I'll call you back to me
The love you gave lives in your little humans' memories
When you think of Momma, as you will often do
You'll know God's love flowed in an angel He sent to you

Bobby E. Hopper
Jemison, AL

Lisa, my wife, and I co-wrote this poem for our dear friend Margaret.

Our 60th High School Reunion

My brother Frank and I graduated the same year; as soon as I heard the news of the reunion my first thought was fear.
I had only three months to lose some weight, but soon learned that was not my fate.
I told my brother I didn't want to go, but he kept after me—he wouldn't take no.
The date finally came; out of town we did go. I'm so glad I went. It was time well spent. Some people I recognized, some I did not. But as far as fun, we had a lot.
It warmed my heart to see my old friends. It was fun to reminisce about times long ago. I looked over at my brother, so handsome and sweet, to see him having so much fun was really so neat.
As the reunion was ending, I found myself not wanting to leave. We said our goodbyes and, yes, there were tears and everyone shouted see you next year.
My first thought was oh great, now I've got to lose some weight.

Rebecca M. Roach
Altamonte Springs, FL

Fade Out All the Doubt

Lord, help me when my soul is in doubt.
Continue to show me what Your love is all about.
Though I confess with my tongue and my mouth
I love You so, but I still battle with doubt.
I know You know my heart is so true.
Help clear my doubt and bring me through
My heart struggles to maintain
In a world of wickedness and shame.
I've seen the hurt and I have lived the pain.
All I ask is when my body and soul seem to fade-out
Come, oh Lord, and save me from doubt.

Amber N. La Fleur
Port Arthur, TX

I would like to dedicate this poem to my five children—my son De'Calus and four daughters, De'Ondra, Clar'Rahnie, Anari, and Anria. I'm just writing the way I feel and I now feel that I have a purpose, a destiny!

The Song of the Wind and Rain

Oh, the song of the wind and rain,
sings of longing and of pain.
It's a mournful, sad refrain.
It's the song of the wind and rain.

Oh, winds why do you blow?
And, whither do you go?
What seeds do you carry to sow?
And from them what may grow?

Oh, rain clouds that obscure the sky,
for what is it that you cry?
Yet soon will your tears run dry,
and let the light return to the sky.

Though things may seem bleak and forlorn,
and there's much that you may mourn,
tomorrow a new day will dawn,
and a brand new hope may be born.

So, sing the song of the wind and rain,
and let it wash away your pain,
until only love and peace remain.
That's the gift of the wind and rain.

Robin Gerhardt-Linkens
Queensbury, NY

Forgive Me

Forgive me for who I am a weak vessel
of humanity upon this life
of learning.
I'm just full of mistakes and
unwanted rules at times.
But as my path shows me the
way, I follow.
Until I find the space where I belong
I must wait and see as one's
mixes of emotions sparks ideas, plants
Brighten lights on the roof of planting
How things must proceed upon
motivating beyond the process of
living.
So if I seem to not walk before
I crawl, don't worry we all get
the hang of it someday.
Just processing this scripture
of knowledge to my poem.
Good luck to all that is on
this one of blossoming upon the
world.

Sendia Gomez Gonzalez
Far Rockaway, NY

Mother of four, one pass and eighteen grandchildren. My passion—painting, writing, creating within ideas. I'm focusing on moving on as life does. With poet, actor SAG Wilfredo Gomez.

Little Brick Church Nestled in the Middle of the Forest

If you listen very closely "Very Closely" you will hear voices singing like angels, music playing that would touch your heart, and make you want to sing along with the beautiful sound coming from this little brick church nestled in the middle of the forest.

As you come closer to this beautiful sound coming from this little church nestled in the forest you will begin to feel a presence of a love and a comfort you have never experienced.

A warm and gentle feeling begins to flow all over you, and as you start to get closer and closer you see a door, and something is pulling at your heart to come even closer and to go ahead and open that door. As you brace yourself to walk up the steps you begin to feel love and the music pouring from behind the door. What kind of feeling you say to yourself is this?

Then I remember as a child when I would go to church and felt these emotions. How the people were loving and kind. The music was so beautiful. The preacher would talk about a person named Jesus being the Son of God and came from Heaven. He loved me and wanted to save me.

I decided to open the door to that little brick church, and I went in, sat down, and started to listen to the words from the man of God. Then the singing and the music was filling my heart and I began to know what was missing in my life, that feeling I had felt as a child and now I have found that feeling again.

Barbara L. Hoover
Nashville, NC

God's Children

They are so kind, with hearts
of gold. I cherish them both their
blessing untold.
Their beauty a light that shines
with style, warming my soul
with their heavenly smiles.
Dr. Gregory D. and Donna Dabov,
you are one of God's children
whom I'm proud to know.

Velmar Pewee Hale Johnson
Jackson, TN

*Dr. Gregory D. and Donna Dabar are the sweetest couple I've had the pleasure of
being aquainted with. May God bless them and keep them well.*

I Love You

My family who has left too soon
You have gone from my sight
But not from my heart or mind
Memories we shared are still here
Prayers of love, peace above
God holds you for now
But soon, I will see you there
Love you all, peace, and rest
My family best.

Jeannie C. Smith
North Little Rock, AR

Come and Go

Times come
Times go
Some with joy
Some with woe
Come and go
Twil always be
We stand
In triumph
We
Never flee
We
Poets of Earth
Hear us breathe

Christine P.
Norwich, CT

Between Spaces

Between spaces,
I am light,
I am dark.
Between spaces,
I am the dream,
I am the nightmare.
Between spaces,
I am camouflaged in the make believe of your world.
Between spaces,
I am old,
I am new.
Between spaces,
 I run,
I fight.
Blending the knowledge of both.
Between spaces,
Which way is right?
Which way is wrong?
Between spaces,
This is where I am misunderstood.

Christy Schroeder
Canyon, TX

This poem reflects the idea that people who suffer severe trauma are typically labeled and misunderstood. The individual does not function as those who have not experienced severe trauma, and it is difficult trying to meet expectations within a judgmental society.

Helping Others

There is always hope for tomorrow
that we will make it through each day.
If we trust faithfully in the Lord above
and try to walk the straight and narrow way.

The Lord will bless us in every way
as we strive to help each other;
to lend a helping hand whenever we can
to make life better for one another.

We can bring joy and happiness
with every kind word and deed we say and do.
It will fill us with a warm feeling inside
knowing the world is a better place for me and you.

Debora Ann Robbins
Temple, TX

Feel Boonie Pain

Boredom makes me be in my feelings.
Like I was running out of time almost every time without an ending.
Oh! How I wish I could run, run, run.
I said to myself, doesn't that sound so dumb, dumb, dumb.
How boredom got me in my feelings.
I'm screaming no more, no more, but there's no place to run.
I went to school to fill my void. Oh no!
My, that was the wrong choice. Didn't know what I was
doing; I about sawed my hand right off. Then I find
myself screaming no way, no way. The boom! Came that
awful snow, trapped and screaming out.
But no one ever comes. Home texting all my friends,
telling them never get trapped up in their house
like what happened to me over and over again.
Signing out, Boonie

Connie Gallimore
Knoxville, TN

This poem is dedicated to my son Tremaine Abrams (Boonie).

Life in Slow Motion

I quit my job to care for you
I gave up a lot of extra activities
I became your caregiving wife
As life took you in slow motion

I started painting the walls
So I wouldn't think about you
Not being here in our house
As life took you in slow motion

I started writing my memoirs
So I could remember the memories
Of us in a better time of life
As life took you in slow motion

I keep the highway hot
Going back and forth to see you
Wanting you to know I love you
As life takes you in slow motion

Lord, I am now asking You
To watch over and protect Rodney
As he is sleeping more and more
As life takes him in slow motion

Peggy Sue Collier
Canyon, TX

I wrote this poem to remind me that Alzheimer's is a slow-progressing disease. My husband has had it for ten plus years. Life has changed for him and me over the last ten plus years. There is nothing we can do but to know that we love each other deeply (even if Rodney cannot voice his love for me at this time) and that our faith in our Lord will get us through this journey as life continues to move forward.

The Cycle of Life

When we're born
We wonder
As tots
We explore
As children
We wish
As teens
We want more
As students
We learn
As adults
We earn
As parents
We hope
As grandparents
We cope
As elders
We pray
For one more day
To wonder...

Patricia Marie Batteate
San Jose, CA

Sunshine

Sunshine you're the light that shines
upon me to warm my body when I'm cold.
Sunshine you shine upon my face
that fills me with happiness when I'm sad.
Using the rain to hide tears in my eyes
from seeing the hate that kills many.
Sunshine you light my way back home
when I am lost in the dark trying to find
my way out of the darkness of hate.
Sunshine you gave a shadow to
accompany me when I feel all alone,
walking by my side.
Sunshine you have put love in my heart
when I had no love at all from within me.
Sunshine your light shine upon all who
are crying from everything they are
going through with the hate, and the eyes
that look at them differently.
Sunshine your sunlight is so beautiful shine,
shine upon all those tears to create
the 7 beautiful colors of the rainbow upon
all and to hold on to living free from all hate.
Let it shine, let it shine, my God let it shine.

Wilfredo J. Gomez
Far Rockaway, NY

SAG actor Wilfredo Gomez, Hispanic-American poet born in Manhattan NY. Raised in East New York Brooklyn. Have two IMDB credit. Cousin of playwright and actor Miguel Pinero Gomez. With six poems published. With Sendia Gonzalez.

Known

How can you be certain
that you know you are right

when your motives are suspect
and your life is a plight.

You gasp when I say this
but you know it is true,

so don't play the victim
because we're all onto you.

I advise to sit silent
and not utter a word,

for you risk being mocked
and being labeled absurd.

Now one final thought—
consider it written in stone—

your choices have consequences
and that's how you are known.

Joe Chmura
Davis, CA

I've been married forty years. We have four children and ten grandchildren. I've done everything from farming, military service, computer operations, construction, working parking garages in San Francisco, and twenty-four years as an optician. My hobbies are playing musical instruments, riding motorcycles, enjoying family, and writing.

INSATIABLE

Feeling your fingers dancing on my flesh
Inhaling your scent
Music seeping into my pores
Sending "your" electricity to my inner core
Giving me a jolt to pure ecstasy
Biting my flesh
Coming alive with you in my blood
Something that has never been endured in my very
Existence!

Concetta Grillo
Brooklyn, NY

Writing poetry since '91, which has been an exhilarating journey putting pen to paper. As years passed, words poured out of me setting my soul, mind, and heart free. I have over 200 poems written and some have been published, which are great achievements that I will forever hold dear to my heart. Having this gift is truly amazing and a blessing all wrapped up in one. My goal is to one day have my very own poetry book published for the world to see. I also enjoy designing holiday dioramas.

Please Listen

I demand
You take my hand.

To walk the land,
Whether it's ice or sand.

All my glands
Will pay the demands!

By trying to write,
If I can't explain the sight.

First it seemed like night,
Then got very bright!

I asked Jesus
To believe us.

About love even when it's rough,
From above, where it's not tough.

'Cause to receive us
is just not enough.

You must show love
From above.

By holding a dove
With a spiritual glove.

David A. Ott
Wapakoneta, OH

Senses of Emergence

I grasp the rough railing,
grateful for the sturdy pine.

Oh! Pungent tomatoes
too long on the vine.

The sight of overgrown roses,
neglected to intertwine.

The crunch of dead leaves,
to my ear divine.

First snow!
Out thrusts my tongue as though I were nine!

I overflow with thankfulness,
my illness no longer to confine!

Deborah Ward Hoglund
Youngsville, NC

Old Church on the Hill

There's an old church on the hill
If you would just go there, you'll get a thrill
There's lots of good old church singing
And a blessing that it is always bringing
The old preacher is always preaching
The Sunday school teacher is always teaching
If you would really like to be a part
Just come on in even before they start
The people are always shaking hands with you
Hoping to get someone coming who is new
Hoping to change someone from old to new
Hoping the change will help them through
Sometimes they have dinner on the ground
Some of the best food that can be found
I know that all preachers like chicken
They say that's what keeps them kicking
The preacher works hard at his job
Trying to change someone who's rough as a cob
The old church doesn't care how you dress
As long as you cover your bottom and your chest
If we would just come to listen to what he has to say
You can bet when it's over you've had a good day

Sam Colburn
Carbon Hill, AL

A Life Rescinded

Oh the sadness, the pain, nothing for gain
Heartache, spirit broken
I went down in flames

Thoughts swirling in my head
Can't return whence I came
Disaster, brokenness, reaching for reasons, why?
Rain falls, faint murmers, no calls

Lift my eyes, still can't see
Why must this agony be?
Those who rescind to saying *no*!
No acceptance of fault. It's frozen in time
in a vault. Precious lives faded
Ne're to love, to dare to live, only upbraided

Helen Higley
Wilmington, NC

This poem was in response to the loss of my son in January, 2023. There are no words to heal. Just time and tears. Easter was helpful—a reminder that Jesus resurrected from the dead and I live for the day we can meet again. I am eighty now and love yard work, decorating our home, and collecting antiques.

Jax

Lucky is the dog who lives with me
They'll have a long life and happy they will be
You'll never be lonely just wait and see
They love you unconditionally, don't you agree?
Ever faithful even when they pass away
They wait patiently near the Rainbow Bridge
Knowing you'll be together again someday
What a glorious reunion that will be
My dog Jax and me

Carol Reeder
Middletown, NY

The Love I Gave Away

I saw saving all the hearts from getting
broke down and lost in my memory.
Cool, calmed and crazy that my life has
never been the same since and now it's
coming full circle.
Again the love I gave away brings a smile
to my face and reassures me that my love
life has its own avenues to follow me
back home.
In my love of return a new place where
I am comfortable and collected.

Theo Tor Carter
Pittsburgh, PA

Blessed by the Best

I was born black, confident, humble
and free.

Loving to inspire others that they
can do all things and believe
like me.

Taking time to appreciate all of
the privileges that I have today.

Thanking the Lord for the gift of
life and doing things His way.

Praising the Lord with songs and praise
because I am blessed by the best
each and every day.

Erasala B. Cody
Tuscaloosa, AL

Youth Train

Hop on the youth train we'll fix you right up
With lotions and potions and all that good stuff
We'll remodel you over from head to toe
So even yourself you won't know
The first is a facelift, then plump up those lips
Straighten your nose and trim down those hips
Fix up your teeth, then work on that smile
Color your hair and give it new style
Slim down that waist a size or two
Hold on, girl, there's more to do
Flatten your tummy and tone up those arms
Shape up those abs and work on your charms
Size up your bust from A to D
Then work on those wobbly bony knock-knees
A brand new wardrobe is last on the list
Your ole duds won't do, they won't even fit
Don't worry about cost we've covered that too
A little ole loan should do the trick
For all that we need to correct and fix
Ten percent down and a five-year plan
To hold you together for another twenty year span
Just sign on the dotted line
Your dreams will come true
A completely overhauled beautiful you

Judy Elaine Rasmussen
Twin Falls, ID

Chosen for Leadership

Mr. Donald J. Trump was chosen
for such a time as this!
This year 2024 we vote for a man
who can put back the pieces of
a shattered America and help
America be great again!
He blessed Israel when he was the
fourty-fifth president; he gave his
time and support that was needed!
Then America was blessed in return!
He proved to each one of us that
he stood for we the people of America!
But still was a peacemaker to each
one he met.
Many years God has blessed America.
It's time we remember,
In God We Trust!

Lois Ann Gassdorf
Rogers, AR

My Gratitude

Through my eyes I want you to see
These experiences that relate to me.
The paths I've traveled to get here;
Stepping stones I've walked through the fear.
Never do we know where we'll end up;
Not always able to see what life's made of.
Now I can choose to view the glass full;
Instead of half empty, stuck in a pool.
No matter my destiny it's never that bad;
Never need to stay down or even stay sad.
I, too, must get up, put a smile on my face;
Know that I can do it and have such grace.
So, if I ever cross a thought in your mind;
Know that our paths met for a time.
It has been my pleasure through and through;
Don't ever forget God blessed me and he has blessed you.

Deborah Meachum
Reed City, MI

Raniyah Lauraie

A tiny little one
Has appeared today
A miraculous gift
Raniyah Lauraie

Her mother's first look
As she lay upon her breast
A love she's never felt
A brand new light in her life

Soft creamy skin and eyes of grey/blue
That flicker with wonder
The wish she waited for was here
Didn't expect to feel this way

Dreams of her future in your mind
A lifetime ahead to enjoy
A radiant glow surrounds her
A sweet angel fills my heart

Margi A. Spurgeon
Glendale, AZ

My granddaughter welcomed her first baby on Feb. 9, 2024. A beautiful baby girl—Raniyah Lauraie. She has been waiting so long to have a baby. Her only heartache is that her grandfather, AKA Tata Larry, was not here to see her. I know he is looking down on her and will forever watch over his new precious great-granddaughter.

Beyond the Chair

There once lived a man of various
talents whose hands were that of a sculptor.
With shears and combs as his tools,
he'd craft his masterpiece with steady
hands that never did falter.

   He gave his talents to many a
client who wore his creations with
pride and confidence. Each client
was welcomed with warm hello's from
miles or more that shared in stories of
joys untold.

   He listened with care as a
confidant and when asked shared
advice. His chair was a sanctuary
of solace where art transformed a
client's appearance, whether a classic
pompadour or a trendy new cut.
His techniques of combs crafted his
art with style and dignity; which left a
legacy beyond his barber chair.

For Family
In honor of Richard J. Normandin

Lisa Fellers
Hays, KS

It's Wrong for Me

I say this
I say that
Some say this
Some say that

But to others
It's alright
But for me
It is wrong

Some do this
Some do that
But if I do
It is wrong

I listen to others
As the talk
They say this
They say that

If I said that
It would be wrong
But right for them
But not for me

Shirley McPherson
Alliance, OH

Remember When

Remember when Thanksgiving
was a happy time.
Mom and Dad and all the kids
together sat down.

Turkey dinner and pumpkin pie.
Every chair filled
at the table
as years went by.

As children grew
and moved away,
some chairs sat empty
on Thanksgiving Day.

Soon more chairs were added
as the family grew.
Small hands gave thanks
as they watched their parents do.

As we age, sorrow comes and goes.
Again chairs sit empty
as we remember the people
who once sat in those.

Jesus is preparing a banquet table.
There will be no empty chairs.
Once again, we will see our loved ones,
for all are invited there.

Sandra Menchio
Westmoreland City, PA

All Alone

All alone thinking of you!
Wishing by the stars that everything I say could come true.
All alone hoping you care. Me calling you by my
side hoping we could share.
A memory together. Just you and me. A memory
together, all alone!

Teresa Favazzo
Ravenna, OH

Musings

But were there yet poetry in me for singing!
There was once, a million years or so ago,
When I was very young.
Life was exciting then,
But less than now with knowing more.
The emphasis has altered though,
And expressions of thought-and-feeling
Are no longer sifted and sung aloud on paper.
This seems a solemn loss somehow
Now the singing's sealed inside,
For time will alter it with new silent songs
And no yellowed reminders of each passing
Will remain to chuckle over at some later date.
Like this.

Jacquelin B. Howe
Athens, GA

Another Year Is Dawning

Another year is ending...but a new one will arrive...
Will this year be a good one or take us to the skies?
In past years we saw simple ways in everything we did
But in these last few years we seem not so very sure.

Gone are the days of carefree thoughts
And having tons of fun...
We leave these days to younger ones...
Our grands we *love* so much.
Remember youth the way it was as we were growing up
These days for youth cannot compare...
To ours without the techs.

The New Year comes to us again... we wish for great rewards
We ask ourselves...will this be one to treasure and afford?
We celebrate New Year's Day for better or for worse...
And pass along our wishes for another year on Earth.
Let's make a pact to all we love...to enjoy our New Year's Day
And look forward to the coming year so full in every way.

So as this year is dawning, Dear Father let it be...
On Earth or else in Heaven another year for Thee.

Martha A. Breakwell
Belle Vernon, PA

When God Speaks

When God speaks, be quiet and listen,
For this is part of being a Christian.
I'm not going to lie, this I am learning,
I want to walk with Jesus like the disciples did, for this I'm yearning.
Oh, I wish I was a mouse in their pocket,
However, Jesus is in my heart and in my locket.
When God speaks, be quiet, be still,
Open your ears and listen for His will.
When God speaks, don't open your mouth,
It's possible that all will go south.

Shannon Louise Young
Jacksonville, AR

I wrote "When God Speaks" on the heels of "The Temple of God." At the time, I felt God inspired me to write that poem. I'm still learning to listen to God, but when I wrote this poem, I felt God was giving me the words to write this poem. I needed only to listen to Him and write.

Perfectly Executed

The planning for our well being
Is always on top of my mind
To prevent misunderstanding
By commencing with a right step

Planification is basic
Performing is something else
Priority is a concern
To accomplish the mission as well

Once the job is done
Happy faces all around
Monies out of the pocket
To pay for a job well done

Perfectly executed is right
By persons of great concern
Capable of doing things
At the maxim of their minds

Raimundo Matos
Spring Hill, FL

It is not what I think, but rather of what I do. Projected things are to be done, regardless of what it cost. A man of action.

Pair Perfection

Kindness is a wonderful thing,
Never forgotten, something to bring.
Always a smile and words so kind,
More positive attitudes are hard to find.

Mattie and Kelly, or Kelly and Mattie,
Professional and helpful is a guarantee.
Never negative or insecure,
Only positive reinforcement is for sure.

Sleep Apnea is a condition to address,
Causing problems of little sleep and stress.
They give guidance and positive tips,
Winning admiration and championships.

In words of closing for this great pair,
Better professionalism has no compare.
A thank you for service, unsurpassed,
For kindness and understanding, always steadfast!

Clay Thompson
Pocatello, ID

In My Garden

In my garden grows seeds of love
Enriched in faith from God above
Seasoned with the Holy Ghost
And planted in the hearts of most

My garden supplies your every need
No room for self unrighteous seeds
The soils the purest God could blend
Cultivated and without sin

God's Holy Spirit flows all around
It nourishes seeds on my garden's ground
The heavenly rain makes growth much better
Then sprout warm love in summer weather

My garden it grows unselfish love
Plentiful in grace from God above
Roots of salvation grow stronger each day
Delivering your soul from its sinful way

God's grace and mercy blooms out each day
For those that's lost and gone astray
His merciful love endures forever
With sufficient grace we're always endeavor

Donald Mathis
Spartanburg, SC

The World

As I sit here underneath this tree watching the leaves
fall over me, I can't believe how beautiful this is,
the world, my life, and things we do to live.
We really don't realize how great it is to be free
to live the life you choose; in some cases you
would never have to lose.
There are so many things to cherish and to do
but where is my life going before this will all be
swept away; I would love to sit here every day
to enjoy my friends, family, and the world around me
but instead I have to see and feel all the evil that
lurks within, for I know we all do sometimes sin.
So I am saying to you look past all the evil and the
hate, for one day we will all think the same.
But until then be yourself and never have any worries
for live life to the fullest and you shall never go
wrong, for happiness is the answer to everything; it is
just the matter of finding the harmony and peace within.

Carrie Lynn Walls
Austin, TX

All Of Me

My mind
Like a shipwrecked shore
Where relentless waves do crash.

Eddie Upchurch
Portsmouth, VA

Great Again

Pro-guns, pro-wall
Pro-life, for all
United we stand
Divided we fall

Stand for the flag
Kneel to the king
Allegiance we pledge
Anthem we sing

To the boys who see combat
For all they go through
For them, we wave proudly
The red, white, and blue

Sofia Arredondo
Sacramento, CA

Truthfully True

From a very young boy you had a heart of gold,
Never one to back down from the original mold.
As you grew years older,
You got so much more bolder.
You were so far ahead from the good and the bad,
And most things never really made you mad.
Always being truthful, honest, and real,
People always knew just how you feel.
No one to mince words of no good,
Every person knew just where you stood.
You walk the walk and you talk the talk,
And never do you ever squawk.
Try not to fault or blunder,
Just never let anyone steal your thunder.
I am blessed to be a grandmother to you,
And that is really truthfully true.

Judy Mitchell
Tarzana, CA

Believe in Miracles

Believe in miracles, they happen every day.
The only thing that stops them is when doubt gets in the way.
Miracles are happening in the midst of pleasure and pain.
They are in every blade of grass, every drop of falling rain.

Your body is a great miracle, each cell knows what to do,
Working in perfect harmony to create the miracle that is you.
Every seed that's planted is a miracle, bringing forth its kind.
And no seeds are more miraculous than those planted in your mind.

Miracles are in the joy of children playing,
In the tender words that young lovers are saying.
In the exquisite song of a chirping bird,
Imagine all the lovely sounds you've ever heard.

Awaken from your slumber to all the miracles around you!
Reflect with a grateful heart on the beauty that surrounds you.
You can recognize miracles when you count blessings amid strife,
For the Creator has woven miracles in every strand of life.

When you look deeply at your life, what do you find?
What do you give attention to with the power of your mind?
You can focus on your fear of what you think you can't do,
Or the glorious promise of miracles that can come true!

Beverly Nader
Fairfield, CT

Fame

You might be well-known
if you are an actor, athlete,
singer, musician, or dancer.

BUT... you are famous
if you are a good, caring
mother;
You are famous if you are a
good, caring father;
You are famous if you are a
passionate, inspiring
educator;
You are famous if you are
a concerned, dedicated
doctor, nurse, or health
care worker;
You are famous if you are a
committed, helpful
policewoman or
policeman;
and...
You are famous if you are a
steadfast, devoted public
servant.

Christopher Winter-Bigney
Wilton Manors, FL

My dear cousin, Kimberly Townsend Palmer, who is also an author, summed up the theme that this free verse poem is trying to convey: "Real fame is all about compassion and action in a world that helps people." As a former educator who has published several children's books and some poetry, I felt compelled to express my idea of what true fame really is.

Forever Is Composed of Nows

Forever whispers, vast and grand,
A concept painted on grains of sand,
But grasp it tight, it slips away,
Leaving only the fleeting day.

For eternity is a distant dream,
A shimmering star, it might seem,
But deep within each fleeting breath,
Forever finds its subtle stealth.

Each sunrise kiss, a brand new start,
Each beat of heart, a work of art,
The laughter shared, the tear that falls,
Let us cherish them, one and all.

Don't seek forever in the far,
It blooms within, where moments are,
Embrace the now, its joy, its pain,
For each "now" whispers, "Live again."

Chase the dreams, hold love's embrace,
Live with passion, leave your trace,
For in the endless sea of nows
Forever finds its endless vows.

Sharon Ann Cunningham
Newhall, CA

As a published poet, I find boundless joy in weaving words that capture the raw emotions we all encounter amidst the tapestry of everyday life. From the gentle whispers of nature to the cacophony of urban streets, I find myriad stimuli that surrounds us. I aspire to transform ordinary moments into heartfelt revelations, inviting others to embrace the beauty and depth found in the ordinary, and to celebrate the profound resonance of being alive.

Light

God is the light of the world
His love is wider than the ocean,
greater than the sky,
over the mountaintops.

He is waiting to embrace us.
We can just accept Him. God never changes,
you can always count on Him.
God would never let you down.

Let the light touch your soul.
Let the light find a home.
Open your heart and let His love grow.
For only God can keep you warm.

The light of God inspired you;
let His light live through you,
let it melt you as you bend your knees,
God will receive you yes indeed.

Nancy Garcia
New York, NY

Reality

Reality kicks in
NYC is the place where home was chosen before the day
Tagged along the birth certificate
Opening my brown eyes from the birthed environment
Years decade
Graffiti sprayed marking the MTA trains
Siren noises countless days
Countless folks different age frames
Voices of personalities
Configuring my instincts
Surroundings of prey
Surroundings of safeguards
Elevation of a mountain view
Where the sun revolves around
Where the moonlight dims
The masters of knowledge
Only the upper stairs of dimension would know.

Lissandra Molina
Bronx, NY

Viewing life through poetry, I've journeyed through self-discovery, finding comfort in verses mirroring my challenges and victories. From youthful innocence to seasoned wisdom, each poetic stanza reveals the resilience, flexibility, and enduring spirit of a New Yorker.

Apologies

You were never good enough
But always better than me
So consumed with lies
I was blind and could not see

Your sacrifices unnoticed
So selfish was I
Everything you did
I would have kissed goodbye

Even though I know better
Twenty years down the line
The guilt is unbearable
Carrying that is mine

There's no way to say I'm sorry
Words are never enough
And what I've put you through
Was more than just rough

Desperate for you to stay
Hope you never go
I know I get the better deal
But you'll never let that show

Jennifer Joyce Moser
Lake Jackson, TX

The Eradication of Luminescence

Of course, I matter not.
As you sow seeds of disparity.
Trivialize my anguish
Delight with wantonness.
Aeonian taunts
Reiterate, reverberate.
Fustigating me further into
Vainglorious self loathing.
As darkness engulfs me
Legions of phantoms
Haunt the corridors.
Lingering, lurking
Ambuscading patiently.
Tick tock, tick tock
Closer, in the garden
Polities are no longer required.
At this point
Does it matter?
Talons embedded deep
Writhing beneath my pellicle
Eradicating potential threats
Piercing my soul
Snuffing out my light.

Gabrielle Leva Nichols
Saginaw, MI

Urban Spotlight

Out of the dark steps a man with a hood
From his hidden place near a great green arch.
There is a lit street lamp near where he stood
In this after-dark park setting, in March.

He looks to the left to see what there is,
Then to the right just to know if it's safe.
This is when a bike passes with a whiz,
And the man turns to the side in a strafe.

He walks, following the way the bike went;
However, the bike was gone—disappeared
Into the night where the cycleway bent.
He strolled 'til the edge of the street's light neared.

Stopping short at the light's perimeter,
A heavy uneasiness seized him fast,
Causing a glance back, making him mutter.
He stares at the dark 'til the feelings passed.

He stands still a moment, highly aware
Of the silent night air all around him.
Tension in his temples, he steps with care—
Vanishes 'til the next street lamp finds him.

Trevor Daniel Otis
Constable, NY

I grew up on my family's dairy farm near the Canadian border, and got serious about writing poetry in college when I took a course in creative writing. Since then I have written a book of poems entitled Dream Deep: A Poetry Collection Based on Dreams. *This poem was written by a fountain pen in a leather-bound journal, both of which were gifted to me last Christmas.*

Mother and "The Six"

Sixty-seventy-eighty years...
What do they reveal?
Mother fixing lunch for us
And cooking her favorite meals.
Father arriving home from work
To eat whatever she has fixed.
Caring, loving, watching us grow,
Cooking, sewing, guiding, teaching,
Sharing whatever she feels we should know.
Oh no! Losing Father, a terrible time for sure!
Mother, you bravely carry on,
Though saddened to the core.
Mother! You're aging, we observe
But "The Six" continue to support and serve.
It's been said one mother can care for many,
And "The Six" say it's the best job of any.
Whether near or far,
We love, no matter where we are
Our mother for all you've done and do!
Sixty-seventy-eighty-now nearing ninety...
Oh Mother!
May love and light continue to shine on you!

Alva Sanders
Riverdale, GA

Damaged People

Damaged people silent screams throughout the midnight
air.
Fathers scold frightened little girls privately down
there.
Mother's physical and verbal pushes him without a care.
Can't have a normal life the damage holds you back.
Tortured souls causing your personality to lack.
The inside pain it goes deep and it's always there.
Destroyed newly formed relations it's never fair.
Turning to drugs that only amplifies the pain.
Wanting so much out of life but you can't obtain.
Damaged people don't get a chance to have wonderful
thoughts.
It's swirling in their brains all the battles they
 have fought.
Their baggage is heavy with no one to help unload.
Damage makes them travel down a dark and broken road.
Misery planted in the deep pockets of the mind.
They can't find a lover or partner of the same kind.
Needing someone to understand that the damage even runs
through their veins.
Cruel and punishing thoughts and actions that keep
the heart in chains.

Lori Lynn Fischer
Fort Walton Bch, FL

Birdsong

As spring begins to melt away the snow,
I think about your garden.
Have you started ordering seeds?
It's been too long since I've been home.

Have you been planning all winter,
Going through seed catalogs,
Making notes and little popsicle stakes?
It's been too long since I've been home.

Have you secretly been picking out flowers?
You know Mom; she's loves them
As much as she loves you.
It's really been too long since I've been home.

As time marches on,
And we're coming up on a year,
The garden has gone to weeds.
But here I am; I made it home.

The bird songs fade into memories,
And every time I close my eyes,
I can see you there, at home,
sitting in your garden.

Deanna Willenbring
Kimball, MN

Two of Our Grandchildren

Izzy is my daughter's baby girl.
To all of us she means the world.
The joy seemed to start when she was born.
Her mother and father had a purpose to
Carry on! Life will never be the same.
When one becomes a parent it changes the
Life game. My daughter now has a baby
Girl and the fact has changed her world.
Jon and Brandy, we envy you. You now
Have a vision of future things to do!
Izzy will seem like a handful for a while.
But one day if you're lucky you'll walk
Her down the aisle. Then we have my son's son.
Oliver is his name. My son's claim to fame.
He follows his father everywhere.
They go up and down the stairs.
Out on the roadway they go. Riding bikes you know!
Out for a bite to eat, dad buys treats!
Oliver is the baby you know.
But each day he seems to grow.
Smart as anyone in the family.
He is a walking library.
Life will have good things for him.
Besides having a great mind,
His father wants him fit and trim.

Clarence G. Underwood
Esparto, CA

Each generation starts life anew. This was true for me and for you. Our lives have been filled with times of joy. First there were children and then grandchildren. The story of the family will continue on even after Grandma and Grandpa are gone. To our family we say thanks for providing us with joy and love! We say this to our children, grandchildren, and all who follow!

Frozen in Time

He was unsure of what to do
Straining to gather his thoughts
Internal words unspoken before raced within his mind
Each one expressed its own reality
Each played out its own emotion
At a speed almost too hard for him to process
The moment had him frozen in time to his core

The sense of fright, happiness, joy, relief, was overwhelming
When he felt he could no longer stand
His arms were filled with a child
Only minutes old, the child also in sensory overload
Each confused as to what to do next
Then they both shared the same emotion
He and his new son crying with tears flowing
Forming a bond for all time

David V. Raacke
Covington, LA

Retired company owner and Vietnam veteran. Poem is an experience of my first born.

My Life

This is my life every day
I know the pain is here to
Stay
It moves around from
Dusk till dawn
It's never really gone
Someday's good
Someday's tears
The good days I get
Stuff done
The days with tears
I rest and sit
Fibromyalgia and
Osteoporosis severe
Doctors say there is
No cure!
Pain, pain go away
Never come again
Another day, this is
My Life!

Pamela R. Sopchik
Caro, MI

The Cry

A cry rang out across the earth
And fled up to the sky;
It traveled to the edge of time
And up to God on high.

The trees paused in their helplessness;
The birds refused to sing.
The earth began to quake and groan,
The hills their rocks did fling.

The light of sun no longer shone,
And flowers bowed their heads.
The wind howled in its misery
No mankind's word was said.

Darkness fell o'er all the earth,
And creatures hid in fear,
Not knowing what was happening,
Calamity seemed near.

The cry was "Father, please forgive,
They know not what they do."
And then the Crier bowed and died,
His plan was carried through.

Margaret Agnes Copley
Aitkin, MN

Shadow Healing

Healing in the shadows
The hidden scars that are always there
That no one can see as they are inconspicuous
She stayed in the shadows trying to stay safe
As she has a hope that they never find her
As she has been through so much to begin with
Healing in the shadows
Seeing the many scars that she has
That she hopes that no one else will ever see
Deep in the shadows is a wounded heart
With so many scars that show the anguish
Everything that she has been through
She sits and cries as she tries to heal
From so much trauma from years past
From so much pain that she thought would be gone
From broken pieces inside
Her courage springs from within
She feels so brave that no one can hurt her anymore
As she feels her heart starting to heal
As this shows her that she can get through anything
As her heart heals, she feels better
Knowing that she can heal in the shadows
She sits there and hopes that
If anyone feels the way that she does
That they know that they can heal
From within the shadows

Laurie Ann Monica Dain
Akron, OH

Why Not Today

Why not today Lord
When I am alive?
Why no acknowledgement while I still strive?
No flowers or phone calls on my special day
No signs of love in any old way

Sweet words of appreciation in my ears never sound
They probably will—when I'm underground.
No reunions or invites, no visits at home
No good mornings or goodnights, just sitting alone.

The singing of praises and words of sweet love
I want to hear *now* Lord; it's what I dream of.
Now is the time because I am still here
So I can use all my senses and enjoy everything dear!

Dora Elia Gonzalez
Harlingen, TX

Awaken

The Father's voice calls
"Wake up" the time of the
rising is come
It's precious to many,
somber to some, but important
to all who will hear.
Listen my children. I will
intruct. Be ready to stand
up and taste of the breakfast
of dawning. The table's prepared.
Come sit come share with the
captured returned.
The victory is ours the
celebration is next but
first we must eat and grow
strong. Chew on the meat remember
to smell and vow never to
sleep thru the call.

Marilyn Droney
Youngstown, OH

This is my fourth or fifth poem sent. I've written "Life's Song," "Ichacar Knows," "The Poem," and now "Awaken." Thank you for this. I'm a wife, mother, and grandmother. I enjoy writing in my spare time as I am led. We are living in unprecedented times. We need to be alert. There is divine providence. I believe we must be sensitive to His promptings.

Not Her

I'm not her
Not the one you use to make her crazy
I'm not her not the fool
Actually, I've learned a lot
I'm not her
You can't come back my patience is gone
I'm not her to believe anything you
    say
I was her, eating up all the lies
    and bull**** you served

Then you showed me your true colors
I've smartened up
Not the one… Not ever again
I'm not her

Tracy Capstraw
Rochester, NY

The Door of No Return

The sky is the same as the day before;
trees taking solace in the wind,
resting on each breeze.
Trees, much taller than the day before;
their strength reaches out to me.
The grass under my feet moves differently,
not guiding me forward; they hesitate,
seeking strength from the earth. I look up.
He knows, "Lord, quiet the water as You did before!"
I am confined, backs never meant to lay down;
now do not know their place, unable to stand.
The taste of dirt settles in my mouth.
Hand lifted are bound unable to feel their strength.
Many are gathered, many different tongues, same fears.
I left the land of my father's, my mother's,
many are to come. They will walk the same dirt;
I know their steps.
I see the sky, the sun as the day before.
I take solace in the wind, resting on each breeze,
knowing never to return.
I see the sky, the sun same as the day before.

Catherine J. Broussard
New Orleans, LA

Catherine Johnson Broussard is an African-American poet and author living in New Orleans, LA. Mrs. Broussard is the author of two books, HIS WORDS, a book of inspirational poems and I Know HIM, a book that focuses on her inner growth.

Friends

What would we do without friends in our life
Friends are with us through fun and strife
Friends are there through thick and thin
Friends are by your side whether we lose or win
Friends pull us up and sometimes down
Friends laugh with us and sometimes give us a frown
Friends are with you through the start
Friends are with you till you depart
All in all, our friends are always there
By our side, all things to share
What does your friendship mean to me
How high the sky, how deep the sea
All these years I can easily say
Friends have gotten me through each and every day

Frances Richter
Saint Louis, MO

I have been writing poems since grade school. I write what I am feeling and for many special occasions and special people. I dedicate this poem to my best friend Lynda. We met in kindergarten and have been best friends for almost seventy-seven years. We are Godmother to each other's son, been in each other's wedding, and been through life and death experiences in each other's family, going through all together.

The Wedding of Michelle and Chaye

Hand in hand this love we share, our vows said
We are now spinning into a grand new era
Of our lives, and I know one of us will navigate
While the other sets sights on the sky as we
Catch one another when the stars come out tonight.

Our whole wide world is in harmony when we
Feel the simplicity of true love and joy we share
The pull of the tides brace one another into
The brazen virtue of the earth where we hold on tight.

The circle of life turns to the tune of our hearts
And I will fly to your stars and jump right in
While letting life's worries fade as we remember
The power of our love.

It is in your arms where refuge and home reside while
Ever in love and thankful for our strong foundation
That holds us grounded within the warmth and strength
Of our heartfelt sighs.

Mariah Ann DeLorenzo
Homeland, CA

I was inspired to write and dedicate this poem to my beautiful cousin Michelle and Chaye when they united in marriage on November 5, 2017 at the Seacliff Country Club in Huntington Beach, CA. It was a perfect day overflowing with love, joy, laughter, and magic.

Technology's Dilemma

Glazed eyes gazing without seeing on every street
Awareness diverted to satisfy instant desire
Enthusiastically grasping varieties of manmade illusion
Dismissing human connections surrendering control to a device
And ignoring inherent presence signaling humanity's retreat
To search for answers to questions that never expire
With acceptance of the progress without recognizing the delusion
As divergent media reports world events with a fear induced vice
Igniting emotions separating every meet and greet
To challenge those spouting truth by every liar
Promoting theories resulting in a community of seclusion
Who can't foresee the danger of AI and streaming apps and the price
Of technology moving forward with blazing headlights
Leaving Earth's future behind in dimming taillights

Raymond H. Murray
New City, NY

You Belong to Me

It's so crazy, in the beginning I
wasn't caught up in getting to know you
thinking you're the same
as the others that were before you
I'm scared, unprepared yet you excite me
though you're not perfect
Perfect doesn't exist
I still want you, flaws and all I insist
I got what you need
You belong to me
We were only meant to be in love
No other man competes
You're just as needing
You know that we'll always be in love
You're all that I need
You belong to me
We're only meant to be in love

Toshia D. Parrish
Tampa, FL

David

David is sitting on his bedroom floor
Staring at the loaded pistol in front of him
While listening to the stereo
Blasting the sound of rock and roll.

Smell of liquor lingering on his breath,
Tears streaming down his cheeks,
He begins to write a letter
For the family left behind—

To his father, a stranger to him,
To his mother, too busy to listen,
To his younger sister, whom he adores.

Life does not matter anymore.
He is alone with no friends at all.
Would they miss him if he was gone
Or forget that he even existed.

He will not find out today.
The alcohol had not overcome
His first instinct to stay alive.

Ann Marie Trimm
Buford, GA

An experience that I would not forget. David took his life at an early age. He was a great young man, brother of one of the youths in the care of an institution. I had to identify his body, which I did not enjoy. I wished that someone had noticed the sign and helped him. Be at peace, David!

Being

Unseen through filters of life
Assumed by one... consumed by another.
It's not unique to me;
I'm a player in the game too.

What am I needed for?
What do I have need of in others?
What do I choose to see?
What do I choose to ignore?

Pure being is an art,
And all art has flaws.
To be thoughtful in a thoughtless world is demanding.
To be artful without thought is impossible.

We all long to be seen in our hiding,
While hiding in fear of being seen.
We all are where we are—
Stranded, unseen, even in our artful expression.

Michael Dale Cook
Greenville, SC

I write in the inspiration of the momentary experience, in hopes of gaining insight and understanding of both self and the human experience.

The Bullied Child

Young but articulate,
Smart and intelligent.
Open-minded with pleasant smiles,
Bringing colors into my files.
Awards received for hard work,
Honors displayed from handiwork!
Looking back to my days at school,
I recalled my sad days of drool,
And bowing low to my undulating emotions,
I regretted not having immediate solutions.
Imagine! Folded papers thrown at me by unseen hands,
And my strangled images pasted on the school boards.
My intelligence was always ridiculed and mocked
By blank non-entities with nothing to be mocked.
Envy glaring openly with jests of a jester,
My successes were opposed with scorn and laughter.
Pushing me from the back was the last unaccepted blow,
With my face disfigured with bumps and without a glow.
Out of frustration, I kicked a silent but innocent bowl,
With the strength of a wounded wolf making a howl.
Straight to my target, the bowl shattered the bully's face,
And an abrupt end came from the bully's space.
My name became an unavoidable quagmire
Of a bullied child who became their nightmare.

Cordelia Chimeziem Ekechi
North Las Vegas, NV

Cup of Coffee

In the past life of a child,
You were nothing more than an attractive annoyance.

In the eyes of a teen,
You were something that crossed my eyes,
A feeble attempt to grasp was made.

Now resting in the soul the man,
I'm glad the red string of fate has attached me to you.
I'm grateful
that it didn't bring over the anger of a boy,
the misguided lust of a teen.

There are a million ways for anyone to say anything.
I thought of them all.
An angel
sent in a time where the void held me in her arms.
There are no words to express the
type of love I feel without it being misunderstood.

So for now I shall sit and wait.
I will forever tell you when you're unsure,
how wonderful you are,
and hope that one day I won't need to speak.
The words will be shown in the picture,
I laboriously paint for you.

Aaron Hooper Jr.
Waterbury, CT

Graveyard

Once I was told my problems were too loud,
That they took up too much room,
And so I did what I knew how, I shrunk them.
They became ghosts almost,
Blinking in every so often to remind me of my guilt,
To tell me that I simply could not be.
My problems loomed over me like monsters,
Like ghosts would do to prove that they are still here.
I would cry myself a graveyard,
Trying to sprout flowers with my tears,
To make my monsters beautiful.
No amount of tears could make my problems beautiful.
And once I was told that I felt too much,
That my affinity to feel was too far, too much.
That it couldn't be dealt with.
And so I did the same thing,
I shrunk my feelings,
I dug so many graves I can't find what I buried inside
And so I just buried myself.
Becoming so fearful of judgment,
I became nothing at all.
And I would cry myself a river,
If I knew which grave I buried my tears in.
All that's left are the buried pieces of me
Littered in my shrunken graveyard.

Paige Stallings
Owensboro, KY

In Case You Forgot

Take a look around—what do you see?
Is it at all what you expected?
Or does misery overpower your glee?
This promised path outlined with love
Only consists of a continuous loop filled with lies.
Because for all that is and all that is not,
I know for certain it isn't what was wished.
So the journey continues full of bumpy and hectic steps.
Many wrong turns with rights that should've been lefts.
You'll encounter this more and more,
While you venture forward on your footpath of life.
So you must always be true to yourself;
Accept nothing that is less than what you deserve.
Be weary of deceit;
Learn to separate the real from the fakes.
Last but not least,
Always keep your eye on the prize.
If you need ask what that might be,
It's the best of the best,
That grand prize is *you!*
For any and all that's scared and confused,
never dim the light that belongs to you.
You are worthy of life and *love!*

Eunice Morgan
Marion, NC

Man in the Moon

So bright and full, shining down,
a beacon to anyone lost in a world of confusion.
Do you know the extent of souls comforted by you?
Eyes gaze upon you at night,
with hopes of guidance, love, relief.
Your stars carry a wish,
a wish that once determined life or death,
cast into the night, but never to be recovered,
gone forever like a penny discarded in a well,
one indistinguishable from the next.
Blackness engulfs the sky, much like the water
that shimmers gold in a wishing well.
What's the difference?
The night turns black
from the disintegration of hope.
The well turns gold
with the inspiration of a new day.
The world is yours to watch at your will.
To instigate love's first kiss,
listen to a porch swing,
or create the mood for an eve of trickery.
When one prays upward, is it you they pray to?
Is it your laugh, smile, or frown that lifts
the head of millions in search for your light?
Or is it false hope creeping through the night,
and chipping away at our increasing hollowness.

Jana Smoot
Colorado Springs, CO

Three Sheets to the Wind

There's fun and frolic now, 'cause we're
Three sheets to the wind
Sailing on the summer breezes
With the sun above us

We're floating through the night
And the stars are shining bright
Reflections of the moon, my lover
Sparkle on the water

This isn't a dream
Although it may seem
Red moon at night—sailor's delight
We've taken to the ocean

We're riding the tide
A heavenly ride
Red skies on fire—our hearts' desire
What a lovely notion

A sweet fantasy, now
Glad you are here with me
We're feeling free, now
Sailing on a blue-green sea

Nina M. Beck
Redondo Beach, CA

Somewhere in Loving You

Father, Savior, Lord and King
Creator of everything
Somewhere in loving You
And You loving me
I fell in love with You

Father, You know I'll do
Whatever You ask me to
I fell in love with You

In all I do
I (I'll) stay close to You
I fell in love with You

When You call my name
(Lord) The way You do
My soul can rest (my Lord) because of You

Hand in hand with You
Wherever You guide me to
I fell in love with You
I fell in love with You

When my life is through
I know I'll be with You
I fell in love with You
I fell in love with You

Somewhere in loving You
And You loving me
I fell in love with You
I fell in, I fell so....I'm in love with You

Becki Jenkins
Lusby, MD

But Not Today

I'd like to go away.
At times it's so hard to stay.
And then I see so much beauty and just have to say, "But not today."
In the early morning light, as darkness breaks away, and the world
awakens all shiny and new. And every possibility can come true.
I look around and say, "But not today."
Standing in a field of sunflowers, my problems just melt away.
And the beauty of those flowers swaying in the wind makes me want to
play and say, "But not today."
As I watch a centipede walk across a log,
I'm in awe of all those legs moving in perfect harmony.
And I marvel at the divine Architect who created such a mystical, magical
creature. And in wonder I say, "But not today."
Walking in a winter wonderland,
the world is once again full of magic and delight,
and in this land of pure white light,
I know everything is going to be all right.
So, to the cascading snow, I say, "But not today."
As I stand before the majesty of the sea and realize the waves were here
long before me and will still be, when I no longer cease to be.
I look into that great abyss and step into the breach.
There I come face to face with eterniity.
And as I feel myself being pulled by the undertow; it would be so easy to
just let go.
But then I look up at the sky and see the seagulls flying high and, in the
distance, there is an explosion of color as the sun melts into the sea.
And I quickly turn back to shore and pray,
Please, God, but not today.

Jane Matti
Moriches, NY

Two Faces

I used to get warm embraces
With my happy-painted faces.
Now the laughter turns to tears;
I have been sad for many years.

In my big shoes, you can see my toes,
But I still have my big red nose.
My clothes are old, torn, and tattered,
But does that all seem to matter?

Please take me to a happier place;
Put a smile back on my face.
My wish is for a Big Top Circus
That would give me a lifelong purpose.

I am going around this big old town.
My smile right now is upside down.
No one likes an ugly frown.
Just let me be a happy clown...

Linda Morrison
Tilden, IL

Just Not Love

I don't know what to say
I love you?
What do I say
To make you stay
Something sweet?
Or something crude?
I love you or I need you?
No matter, you don't care
You see no love for me
Though I'd die for you
How come you don't want me?
When I clearly yearn for you?
Am I too tall? Or is my hair just not right?
I love you with everything I am.
Though you love me like a common cold.

Duncan Horsechief
Miami, OK

Hello! I'm a sixteen almost seventeen-year-old author and poet. I struggle with the plague of being a hopeless romantic; sometimes it's too much and my writing helps with it.

Grasping at Stars

No matter what I do
No matter what I say
I will always be chasing
The feeling that I can't help
I try to make a shining star
Shine brighter than before
It will always be dulled
By those there before
How can I show
That not just one
But more
Will always be polished
In the beautiful star
That was there before
Many have come
To see it shine
I will cherish all that are there
Shining in my palm

Lisa Koehler
Douglas City, CA

One

When I'm on a hill
In a swing on a tree,
How can God see me?
How can God see me?
One little girl in a big,
Busy world!
How in the world can it be?
How can God see me?

My grandma says,
God made us all
And His spirit is near us from birth.
For home He made and gave to us
This amazing earth!

Our heavenly Father knows all
From His glorious home above.
God sees each one with love.

Marilyn Cox
Rural Hall, NC

I Once Was a Bird

I once was a bird.
At times I can still feel
what it was like to fly like one,
in the wild, soaring above borders…

But I died, and returned,
as prisoner in this body, this shell,
suffering claustrophobia from having
too good a memory and a profound inability
to tolerate the tiny cell that holds my physical self.

I now think of death not as another incarceration
nor extermination, but rather as a consoling liberation
because this singing-thing within will be free to fly again.
And I won't look back with longing once I've fled. I will catch

                                                                  gone

                                and be

                           higher,

                    higher,

my old friend the wind and soar

Arthur Feinsod
Santa Fe, NM

Home

They say home is where the heart is
A white picket fence living in bliss
A mom, dad, sister, and brother
Under one roof, living together
Whether we laugh, cry, have good days or bad
We love each other and it's a treasure to have
Home will forever be where the heart belongs
And even if you've never had one
It's never too late to create your own
Foundations are the key to a life of abundance
Which is exactly what a home provides us

Sheneka Mackson
Houston, TX

I wrote this poem because I've never experienced what a real home looks or feels like, but I imagine it's something like this. We all need homes that create a foundation of love and trust because, with how cruel the world is, going home to your family should provide you peace of mind from it all.

Echos in the Void

The sky is dark
Except for a faint hue of deep purple above the hills.
A tree's black silhouette is barely visible.
The cricket decides to call out.
"Hello," it says with eagerness.
"Hello," another calls back.
A friend! How wondrous.
Sometimes the darkest moments
Are where light shines brightest.
The cricket says, "It is nice not being alone."
The other responded in precise agreement.
A single companion, unseen but not unheard.
Nearby, somewhere along the stone wall.
Patient, but diligent.
Doesn't start, but always finishes.
Never creates, only echoes....

Morning bird take me away.

Samuel Hopfe
Englewood, CO

I wrote this poem while sitting outside my house, listening to the crickets chirping.

Milo

The first day that I laid eyes on you,
I felt your love and then I knew.
We would always be together and never blue.
In your 10 short years you have made my life full.
I will never forget and I will always love you.

Terri Allen
Colorado Springs, CO

I Want To

I want to soar high in the air.
I want to fly above the clouds.
I want to fly and reach for the sun.
When I try to fly higher,
My broken, tethered feathers don't carry me.
I cry and fall down.
I look at my wings, they are bare and scarred.
O' God take me high in the sky to fly to You.
Reach out so I can see and touch You.
Take me home, so I can rest, heal, and feel safe.
I am tired of fighting the storms; I hurt all over.
I am tired of flapping; I look around and I am alone.
With no light in sight, just cold and darkness.
O' God take me home.

Jason Pruden
Sandy, OR

Could've Been Worse

Are we here to live
or live in fear?
What's the differrence
is what I hear.
I've been through lots
but could've been worse.
I'm still here
and not in a hearse.

Erin Canady-Denham
Puyallup, WA

Erin Canady-Denham started writing in the 1990s and attended college on a vocal scholarship. Over the years, she's been published multiple times. In 2021, she won a romance short story award with TCK Publishing. She was published in Eber & Wein's book, Best Poets of 2022, and Who's Who in American Poetry 2023. A book of her poetry along with her own artwork was published with BookLeaf Publishing in 2023, Life is an Adventure. She's a cancer survivor and RN but her greatest accomplishment in life will always be her United States Marine veteran son.

Bird's-eye View

My comfort zone is unknown before I knew it.
I was there reviewing the moment.
It was so fast, a flash and a dash.
No wonder no one saw me. I was a ghost on scene.
But it's me—the girl in your dreams.
I could clearly see me. You can't see me.
I, hence, change a fog perhaps different
heavy mercury fog.
It's coming. I could almost touch it.
I know it's a gloomy feeling.
Heart beating fast, I hear thunder, I see a flash.
I fly way!
I found a cave; l wonder which way l go?
Is there freedom beside these mountains?
l question the path l leap.
l awaken here. l am exalted from the dark depth's
wooded area.
I landed. I wait. No one is near.
Impossible how no one sees me—l am right here,
tweaking songs near an open fire.
Don't you see l am standing right here with a broken wing
near the fire.
l was here.

Jennifer Bastedo
Paisley, FL

I Just Want to Cook and Wash Dishes

Today, I turned eighty-three just as happy as can be.
But then my husband up and died.
My son started making such a fuss;
you will come to live with us.
So, they packed me up and moved me to their home.
Believing they want and need me,
what an adventure this will be, to live in
a house full of kids, dogs, and fleas.
It's only natural that I would want to help out;
I certainly don't want to just sit on the couch.
To my surprise,
when I realized, I was in the way of their busy lives.
All I want to do is cook and wash dishes;
let me do something for goodness sake.
Oh, Mom, you don't have to do that anymore;
take it easy, they would say,
we have a maid that comes in every day.
If I could only go back home,
I would not feel so alone!

Alisha Boettger
Conroe, TX

This poem represents the thousands of senior citizens who have been invited to move into their children's homes and are quickly pushed aside for countless reasons and because they were not in their home, they didn't feel free to move about doing their own thing. Most seniors need a purpose, and they need to feel needed in order to be happy and healthy.

Following the Light

Quickly
    Time passes by me faster than I realize
You and I will never share more than what we do now
Never our souls
    Always the nutrients that flow between our roots

Sighs escape my leaves and I grow, passing you by
I never asked you to give up your essentials for me
    I love that you love me

In the end, here is what I know:
Clouds taste like imagination
    Mimicking the colors of the sun
Wind is the finest major triad chord there is
    Harmony sounds like it feels
I will never be content with the sky I've touched
    Always reach for more
None of that matters if you aren't here to share it
    Water will never quench the thirst I have for you

I will wait for you to take my hand and follow me

Marinah Inman
Hartford, WI

Inevitable

Stripes of frost between which sun
through branches melts.
Melts because frost is fleeting and sun is prompt.
The stripes are inlets no light touches, the frost
settles and clings and squeezes, thin green blades
choking beneath.
The sun reaches her climax and the stripes succumb, but
two years later, streaks of beige stain
the healthy earth, paralleling stripes of bark still
towering above them.
Did the branches plan to kill slowly?
Did the stripes beg for a swift end?
Does the unmarred grass remember?
If you squint from far away on an autumn morning,
it's an ocean of green glitter.
If you look closely that same afternoon,
it's a cemetery, with live mourners all in green.

McKenna Kjelshus
Newnan, GA

Ruby Rock

On my way to Ruby Rock
I slipped
Tumbled down
Smashed my head open
On the rocks
My body
Crashing with the waves
Where they make their white crests
Pulling me into the Atlantic
They will mark it at the point
Where I slipped
Like the kid on Fox Island
Where the Kennebec meets the Atlantic
See me go out
Struggling with the tide
The saltwater in my mouth
Choking
Smashing against the rocks
Head burst open
In a red tide
At Popham Beach
People point at it
Screaming
From their cottages
They will mark the point at Ruby Rock
Where I slipped

Jonathon Dye
Worthington, OH

Dream Entities

Here, again, I find myself
So suddenly stuck in time.

Wandering all around
With my ever-wondering eye.

Then I feel the sky come down
As if She wants to feel me breathe,

Setting free my anxiety
And reminding me
To not fear sleep.

Griffin Mergele
Streamwood, IL

I'm unsure if I believe in any specific religion. But I've had unexplainable religious experiences that have felt like a comforting hug in times of turmoil. And I turn to those memories when I need reassurance that things will be okay.

Footprints

I was always told to act like a role model for you
In reality I followed your steps

Being told I'm going down the wrong path
But you were always at the end waiting for me

Shouting I hate you and how I can't wait to leave
But crying realizing one day you'll be the one to go

Realizing I don't have many friends
Then look down the hall to see my forever one

Seeing you cry hurts more than cuts
If I could heal your heart, I would in an instant

They say growing up is a gift
Watching you grow is the best gift of all

What happens when my steps wither
You'll be the footprints I keep on following

My life
Was never really my own

To my sisters
My footprints are really just yours

Darianna Moschetto
Allenstown, NH

To My Sisters, I Love You

Good Morning, Spring

Listen to the ballad of the birds
as they sing their ancestors' songs.
Hear the ripples of the river
as it whispers words of wisdom.

Feel the brush of the breeze
with strokes so soft on your skin.
Embrace the solace of the sun,
its warm rays wrapped around you.

Watch as the flowers grow full,
blooming like smiles in the sunshine.
Witness the colors of the sky
as day fades into night.

Stop, pause, look around
and experience the things
which are most profound.

Hailey Metzger
Louisville, OH

Tomorrow

The sun sets,
Soon to rise and begin a new day,
So all sins will be washed away.
The guilt, the shame, the disappointments,
They do not exist in the land of tomorrow.
Tomorrow does not accept carry-ons;
Heavy luggage costs extra.
Tomorrow is tropical,
Full of transparent water and calm waves.
Tomorrow is galactic,
Full of stars, unexplored planets, mysteries—
Inexplicable, beautiful things.
Tomorrow is a seed blown off a dandelion,
Drifitng in the wind,
Its destiny and destination unknown.
Tomorrow is when the sun sets,
Soon to rise once again.

Abigail Grisham
Littleton, CO

Paradox of a Mother's Grief

Sometimes I see you
Dancing in a princess dress in my dreams
In the upturn of your brother's smile
In the shiny white scar on my belly
You reflect off every sequence, every sparkle
I can see your dimples, hear your laugh
Feel your tiny hand wrapped around my thumb

And sometimes I don't see you
I can't picture the exact color of your eyes
I forget the way you smell
I can't recall the sound of "momma"
A distant label that no longer fits
Like trying to pull on jeans spun around and around in the dryer

And I hate myself for not being able to button them
I hate myself
For all the times I fall apart
For the memories that are too sharp and crisp they cut me
For the memories I've misplaced like an unimportant extra set of keys
And for all the ways remembering breaks me
And for all the ways I've failed to remember
You

Jamie Peterson
Irvine, CA

Unusual Life

I have loved and I have been loved
I have visited the vast land of imagination and dreams
I have kissed the unkissable and I have been kissed
I have cried tears of joy and tears of pain
I learned about this galaxy
and hoped for other worlds beyond it
I saw what is yet to be seen
and saw what has been there all along
I have smelt the burning truth
and I have tasted the innocent lies
I have savored life, death, and everything in between
I have been humbled and I have been arrogant
I have felt what it's like to soar above the sky
into the heavens and felt what its like to
crumble into the pits of hell
I have heard the ones who are not meant to be heard
and I heard the loud voices of others screams
I have waited for the mystery of the dying world
and I have been given hope for the beginning
I have the blessing of this world
and I have been cursed to live within it
I have lived the most unusual life

Rawan Bouvier
Houston, TX

Memories of You

A warm hug, a smiling face
memories that others try to erase.
The color green and bad jokes,
those are the memories I love the most.
Morning hello's and evening calls.
Saying that you loved me, was best of all.
I was your favorite, your loving granddaughter,
and you, my Abuelo, my best grandfather.
Everything was perfect, nothing could change.
Until your memory started fading away.
I guess that old saying is very true.
"If you love someone, you have to let them go," too.
I had to end the chats and evening calls.
For the sake of myself, my family, and you most of all.
Now, it's been a few years,
and I'd do anything for one more hug,
and no more tears.
I love him so much, and it broke me from the start,
but he'll always be with me, forever in my heart.

Serenitymarie Sanchez-Lopez
Summerville, SC

In Due Time

My eyes scorched from today's light,
I look around,
in between the flames,
I don't see life.
Where are the birds?
Do they cease to fly?
My ears muffled from today's lies,
I listen,
in between the cries,
I don't hear life.
Where are the birds?
Do they cease to sing?
When I held myself in isolation,
while destructive,
I had the best of intentions;
hence, I've lost all of my senses.
I'm no more dead than alive
but in due time,
I might survive.

Emily Snyder
White, GA

Spirit Guide

You taught me to widen my focus
You taught me to open my eyes
You showed me there is more to see
You opened my mind to what might be

You brought goodness into my life
You showed me the goodness already there
You have altered my perspective
You showed me many ways to care

You continue to challenge and question
You show me what I see is not all there is
You have helped me understand who I am
You really just made me give a damn

If I haven't told you already
I want to say it now
Thank you for everything you've shown me
For giving me my Tao

Katharine Hale
Durham, NC

I am a Tao Student of Life, always searching for what is out there and why are we here? As such I endeavor to understand my life within this world and beyond. I have been lucky to find a few individuals who have helped me expand my horizons and wrote this poem as a tribute to them.

Pisces Moons

You and I are Pisces Moons—
Whimsical. Empathic. Compassionate.
Full of life, always here, there, and everywhere
for our families. Friends. Loved ones. Whenever
and wherever they need us. We show up for one
another in all our friendships. Relationships.
Partnerships. Whether we encounter our siblings.
Colleagues. Or best friends, we go out of
our way and often set ourselves on fire to keep
the ones we love warm.

You and I are Pisces Moons. We
get each other. We see each other for
who we truly are: beautiful. Intelligent.
Wonderful. Both outside and within.
We let our intuition and emotions guide
us through our lives and partnership.

You and I are Pisces Moons—it didn't work
out romantically between us and other
people. They don't understand us; perhaps
we do. So, my fellow Pisces Moon, let's give
this thing a go. After all, what do we have to lose?

Julia St. Clair
Scarsdale, NY

This poem is dedicated to my "fellow Pisces Moon." Although he said he loved me, he chose someone else. If God and love want us to be together He'll reunite us in divine timing.

Bruises

the bruises adorn you like a crown of jewels
amethyst
topaz
declaring that you refuse to back down

when the world pushes you to your knees
rise
bare pearled teeth
let rubies spill from scraped skin

lessons more valuable than diamonds
gold
nothing more glorious than head held high
perfect crown of perseverance

Bailey Cory
Bondurant, IA

The true measure of character is not success, but perseverance through adversity. "Bruises" is an ode to this tenet which I live my life by.

Your Ocean

seas wrap around my lungs, salt piercing my wounds as i
drown she pulls me down, with the wrecks around
her screams echo through my ears, mine can't take
anymore of their screams as i jump into the depths
beneath me; surrounding memories of you wash in.
the beach absorbs your kindness, as she sings a tune
you were gone too soon. blue and grey messages pop
through water. does water have a different meaning?
maybe it does, maybe it's you, so beautiful, resilient
and powerful no one could control you or her. we
couldn't keep you from her grasp. the sea still
absorbing my tears, taking my pleas. your rain fills
her body, my tears fill her body as she takes and she
takes more as she breaks and she breaks me more.
the sea won't take me, won't let me join you
she takes everyone but me even while i beg to be taken,
i beg to feel no more pain but she deposits me onto the
sand back where there's sea glass and critters, litter
and broken shells. you're not there anymore, no pain.
no crying, nothing to cause pain. waving from the
horizon, smiling. your curls defined by moonlight.
stardust collecting at the bottom of the ground and my
tears stand on sand. are you in the heavens now?
instead of stardust are you the stars? instead of stars
are you still rain? rain that comes on a sunny day,
creating rainbows in your wake.

Kyle Alberg
Smithfield, RI

*I wrote this poem very differently than how it has been written here but the meaning
of it still rings true. I wrote this poem the day my music teacher passed away. She
was a beautiful and amazing woman, the type of person you could never find a
negative thing about. I had found out she passed away shortly after Christmas
near New Year's Eve which was an incredibly difficult process to go through at the
start of the new year. One could compare it to drowning in the ocean.*

You

"How are you?"
I speak, ask, but I feel silent,
A cold hand covering my mouth,
Trapping my words, my feelings, me,
The encroaching nothingness.
"How are you?"
The haunting loneliness surrounding me, waiting,
Holding my thumb to the screen, typing, to you.
"Are you doing okay?"
Your need, your attention,
Choking my words, unheard, my cry for help.
"Are you okay?"
I paid it forward, the ask, the care,
Deposited into a safe that takes and takes,
Bad investments returned in a dark spiral of winter,
You,
Don't you see?
Don't you care?
Please, can't you notice? I need you, You.
You laugh and point, You correct,
You push me to my breaking point and past it.
What do you want from me?
Why am I still here, by you?

"How are you?"

Morgan Pletcher
Arlington, VA

In the Wet, Black Dirt

bare-fingered oaks tangle
the way the tumor burrows.

Past the fields on 95N,
you say I love you,

a prayer.

Bless me, Father,
though your voice is hoarse.

Windows down,
we let in the storm;

tilled earth and rain.

Joyce Deuley
Bertram, TX

Burning House

I don't know why I long to feel love
but I cut off every limb it touches.
When you get hurt at a young age, you learn to carry
your pain the way a child carries a teddy bear.
The pain comes back like nostalgia
and I end up alone like I always do.
When you've been charred, you don't mind
running back into a burning house; it's strange
how we find comfort in the people who hurt us.
It's a different kind of loss
to be shunned by the thing that once saved you.

I hate that I care for people
who wouldn't even think to care for me.
I hate that I've come to terms with winter,
when I deserve to be loved like spring.
I hate that if I were offered a sweater,
I would choose to freeze.
I hate that this desolation
is starting to feel like peace.

I fear that if I could feel love,
it would've touched me by now. I could put out
a fire with all these tears that I cry,
but when you get hurt at a young age,
you learn to feel at home in a burning house.

Helene Coberly
Papillion, NE

Helene G. is a twenty-year-old writer from Nebraska. She works as a behavior therapist and enjoys doing what few things the Midwest has to offer, such as driving aimlessly for hours while listening to music or going for leisurely strolls through the aisles of Target. For more of her work, check out her poetry anthology.

If Heaven Had a Phone

If Heaven had a phone
I would call you every day
I would start with, "I love you"
and "How was your day today?"

If Heaven had a phone
I would call and let you know
of all the things you missed,
since you had to go.

If Heaven had a phone
I would be so very happy.
I wouldn't have to curse and scream;
it makes me feel so crappy!

If Heaven had a phone
I would be so at ease.
I would be less stressed and anxious
knowing I could call you as I pleased.

But Heaven doesn't have a phone
and that makes me so sad.
So I guess you have to wait on me;
I love and miss you, Dad!

Justin Ann Meager
Neffs, OH

Woe to the Complacent

History is repeating itself,
but it seems everyone is too blind to see.
A sleeping monster is lying in wait,
like a bear being poked with annoying little jabs,
its annoyance simmering until it finally builds to rage.
The monster will wake and it will be too late to stop
the destruction that is sure to come,
because a dictator has cleverly positioned himself
as he waits to take the reigns of the beast,
stealthily lead it to destroy everything in its path
like the Narcissist savior he is.
Only it's a move that has been spoken of before,
a move our true Savior has warned us of.
We must not sleep, but keep our eyes and ears open
so that we are not blind when the time comes
For us to meet up with our Savior in the clouds
Until that time we must be patient.
Conquer hate with love.
Humbly give help to those in need.
Don't blindly believe every lie placed before us.
Instead, shine bright, love one another,
and know that our Lord Jesus Christ is watching over us,
waiting patiently to welcome us into,
our forever home.

Leslie James
Tulsa, OK

Nevertheless, Spring Is Near

The December air cast a spell on the trees.
Little by little, their leaves and color faded away.
Left with nothing but sticks, the bare trees
Performed their job with grace and elegance.

However, the tree was ashamed.
"What shall they think of me?" It thought.
Yet, regardless of its shame, the tree continued
To serve as a home for the animals.
It provided shelter and gave birth to life.
In another season, the tree will gain back its color.

Nevertheless, regardless of how you may feel,
You have a job and a purpose to fulfill.
Do not neglect that purpose.

Like the naked tree, you, too,
Will attain those bright colors.

Don't give up just yet;
Spring is just around the corner.

Nadia Tubbs
Fayetteville, NC

Anything But That

In the depths of love, a sea so wild,
Merciless waves like a tempest beguiled.
Drowning in passion, the best of ways,
Yet, you crave anything but my gaze.
My love, an ocean, a tidal spat.
You'd want anything but that.
Hollowed my heart, your shelter, your own,
Too much love, seeds of longing sown.
I'd sculpt my soul, a vessel for you,
In the hollows our love is renewed.
Yet, too intense, my love's array,
Anything but that, you'd gently say.
Yearning for solace, a different track,
In this symphony, anything but that.
Colors of emotion, a palette untold,
In the verses of love, our story unfolds.
But you resist the waves, the tides so vast,
Anything but that, a wish steadfast.
My love, a force, too grand to bear,
Yet, you seek solace, a tranquil air.
In the silence, echoes of your plea,
Anything but that, a melody set free.
Anything but that, your refrain,
A heart too full, a love to gain.
Yet in the echoes of this lyrical spat,
You'd want anything but that.

Kontessa Payne
Avoca, NY

Lake Havasu

Wading in the water
far out, so I could truly be alone

I submerged myself
yellow bikini and all
into the murk

I came up baptized

not a Christian
not a Catholic
something stronger

the car ride there was my pilgrimage
and the music we listened to were like hymns

the sand that stuck to my body
was a welcomed gift

and I returned home
smelling of spikenard

the sunburn that peeled
reminded me I was real
and for that I am grateful
to Lake Havasu

Atticus Dalton
Flagstaff, AZ

I've been writing ever since I could remember. It's always been a passion of mine. It wasn't until high school that I discovered a love of poetry. I thought it was pretentious and too structured. But I quickly learned it didn't have to be that way. And ever since then, it seems to be I've been writing more or less non-stop. I hope to continue my writing in the future, both on a personal level as well as a professional one.

Mother, Now I Know You

You were a little girl born in, Tylertown, MS.
When segregation was prevalent, and in 8 years
your loving father was taken from you,
on a New Year's Day, in 1950, (@ 12 am).
What a violent memory to hold so dear.

He was a homicide victim of a jealous foe, a queer
cousin I'm told, was enticing your mother to lay with
him, but your father resisted his advances on her
behalf, and he was shot in the chest at
point blank range.

What a somber moment for an 8-year-old little girl.
That year the New Year was no longer new, but had
become old to a now fatherless you.

Shrell Jenkins
Kingsville, TX

Death of Words

My finger is a graveyard of unspoken words
words that belong in a story
words about birds singing as they fly
as they fly off to Neverland
Neverland is where missing children go off to

Skeletons dancing on their graves
their heads moving forwards, backwards
as the night falls upon them
When the sun rises, they are gone

People opening doors for others
laughter of silly jokes
jokes about how Karen stole the kids
of lost hope, death of animals

All things that were once written
written for a story but eventually gone
gone after edits, and edits, and more edits
All could be part of a story, but none will ever know

Arianna Trent
Califon, NJ

Fear

In the fading kiss of twilight,
harkened by the shadows creeping out of the dark crevices
once lit with the brightness of day.

Shackled by my past, unable to break free, I look for a dim path
leading to an unknown future.

My mind seeks solace from the cold phantoms creeping
amongst the blackness of night, siphoning every ounce of my
existing sanity. The eerie silence holds me in its withered
fingers as ransom to the terrors of the dark abyss.

My mind races to make sense of the forms from my past.
Finding none, my body shudders at every thought as I tearfully
turn to hide my face. Lost in the fleeting moments, I find myself
succumbing to fear that surrounds me.

Alexander J. Shadikhan
Aurora, IL

Blood on My Sheets

Even as I sleep,
my body rejects the womanhood that pours out of me.
A man possessed,
I search for him in that gaping wound
between monochromatic visions
splattering against the windshield of what I call
me.
Reminding of things forgotten;
pink wallpaper with sparkles,
embedded like the blood caked in my nails.
The reek of my mother's cigarettes;
wet, rotting carpet,
the mouthpiece between my legs.
With yellow teeth she speaks of want, of need, of ache.
Of the things I bury to maintain control.
Of the things my mother flouted.
Chubby fingers not yet petrified with blood
dancing on black and white ivory.
The same piece, again and again.
The same vision,
again and again.
The same bloody itch I reach knuckle deep to scratch,
to chase,
to clutch the high of masculinity.

A. N. Anderson
Auburn, MA

Halfway

Halfway,
Promising never to go astray.
Halfway,
Healing, emotion, and play.

Light eyes,
Lovers feel alive.
Recognize,
Serendipity and compromise.
Sacrifice,
To survive to be precise.

One day,
Our light turned to gray.
Betray,
Think before you say.
Today,
All I can do is pray.

Halfway,
That's where to meet me, if you may.
Halfway,
Before you walk away.

Robert Wilson
Prescott, AZ

Ellipsis

Isolation induced by forces unforeseen
Once twins from separate wombs now halves divided
Depths tested without perception
Only lunging into darkness

Alone feels cold. Quiet.
No broken silence filled with purple laughter
If this broken union were punctuation it would be...
Waiting for the next lines to be written

What you were once banned from brought you back to me
The next lines are being written one text at a time
Euphoria is slowly eclipsed with a twinge of sonder
We're not ten anymore

We wear new clothes accommodating to brand new styles
And we both have dogs the other doesn't recognize...

Anna Pulsifer
Whitefish, MT

I wrote this poem for anyone who had a best friend whom you were separated from by external forces, things out of your control. It's a sentiment to all of those years spent apart and finally getting back in touch and realizing just how much has changed; everything from the clothes you wear to your dogs. It's a bittersweet feeling to have something you valued so much, but it hurts when you know it will never be the same. So, if you have also experienced a similar situation, you're not alone.

Confession

I confess.
The father I knew isn't the father I know.
And although his smile is the same
And we share the same surname,
I think he's insane,
Something lost in the brain
For leaving this way.
Paused at the peak of my adolescence.
Missed my homecoming,
Thanksgiving,
Birthday,
And every day in between.
Who burns a book when they reach chapter two?
Apparently, you.
You didn't even get the chance to read the summary.
And now I'm stuck reminiscing a fantasy.

Annabel McIntosh
Chicago, IL

I had a rather unusual upbringing. I grew up in a happy family until my father left when I was thirteen. I found a safe place in writing poetry because it was the only way I could express my feelings and emotions during that difficult time. My first poetry competition submission gave me a newfound sense of pride in my writing and in sharing the poetry that I had been hiding. I find that poetry has saved me. And I hope that my experience and writing can influence other teenagers to put into words what they keep hidden inside.

Her Mask

Every morning she applies her mask
A facade so no one sees who she truly is
Everyone thinks she's someone else
She's been faking perfection for so long

She wears foundation
To hide her tear-stained cheek
So no one sees how much she's hurting

She wears concealer
To fill in the trenches that dug underneath her eyes
So no one sees her sleepless nights

She wears mascara
To distract from what hides inside her eyes
So no one sees her wall of pain

She wears blush
To trick everyone into believing she's happy
So no one sees her colorless face

When no one's looking she takes off her mask
She thinks no one would love her if they saw
I wish she knew she could drop the act
Because I love her without the mask.

Caela Kushner
Guilderland, NY

I'm Caela Kushner, a fifteen-year-old poet from upstate New York. I wrote this poem as a love letter to the women who feel like they need to conceal who they are. I want you to know that I can see you behind the mask, and I love you anyways. I love you with or without the mask, and I know that others will, too.

Broken, or Fixed?

I was the broken package on his doorstep,
Yet he brought me back in.
Into his deep green eyes I fell.
Fell back into the regular routine.
He kissed me, then the ring came back on my finger.
Finger that longs to be non-existent.
We were happy.
Until my secret emerged.
Emerged from the one I thought I could trust.
Trust fell between me and my lover.
He who loved me, or so he said.
Said that we now would sleep in separate beds.
Bed that now seems lonely without him by my side.
His body that comforted me in the night.
Night where he came in again, took me in his arms.
Again, the new routine came, but so did the question.
The question about my heart:
Broken or fixed?

Olivia Bryant
Murfreesboro, TN

Hello! I'm Olivia, and I love writing any sort of romantic poetry. One of my recent poems, "My Dear," was inspired by my sweetheart, but this one is special. Inspired by a book I recently read, I knew it was the right one. A special shout-out to my parents, my two best girlfriends, Avonlea and Olivia H., and my three best guy friends, Colin, Joseph, and Luke. They daily encourage, joke, laugh, and grow with me. This wouldn't be the same poem without any of them. Thanks for reading, and keep an eye out for my work on shelves!

The Meeting

I believe every parent
has anticipated
and speculated
the meeting.
Nine months is a long time
to select and reflect names,
change room ideas,
and dream of the future.
Every birthday
every holiday
every special moment is possible
because of the meeting.
I remember a rainy crisp
fall morning
when we became parents
for the first time.
An introduction wasn't necessary;
you knew us instantly.
The encounter would last a lifetime—
a lot of lessons,
a lot of memories.
So, here the two of you are
about to take the journey to parenthood.
It all begins
with
the meeting.

Keith Jefferson
Walbridge, OH

Coping

Getting that news all you can pray for is more time
But they were gone in a blink of an eye
Deep down you know it is already too late
They are gone and you have to accept the fate
There is so many feelings that come with death
It is to hard to believe they took their last breath
Coping with the pain is something you will learn
Remember God has not made it your turn
But trying to be positive can be very hard
Especially when the pain can leave you so scarred
Death can be something you sometimes do not understand
Until you're in that moment experiencing it first hand
Even on your hardest days remember you cannot quit
You have to just try and continue working through it
There may be days you get lost in your thoughts
They may even leave your stomach in knots
Losing someone can do something to your heart
How can it not? Sometimes it can even tear you apart
Giving up will seem like the answer to it all
You shut everyone out and put up a wall
Doing that will only put you in a even darker place
Eventually that loss... you will have to face
The best way to deal with the pain can be unknown
But one thing you should not do is deal with it alone
Even when it gets to hard just make the choice to stay
"I need help" are words that are okay to say

Nailah Jones
Monongahela, PA

I started writing in the beginning of 2022 after losing my sister in December of 2021. Writing was one of the biggest things that has helped me with losing her. Poetry has let me express the things I keep inside, being open with my emotions and feelings was something that was never easy for me. After I started writing I actually started to feel some comfort with the loss of her. Getting into writing was probably one of the best things I ever did.

A Chance for Ordinary

Can you see the beauty
Although it seems quite simple
In how the snow sparkles
Under the streetlight
After dark
Dancing to the ground
Under the illuminant spotlight
A heavenly performance
With no audience to marvel
At their elegant movements
Turns, twirls, and spins
All for not a soul
But the ones who dare to look around
Who give the ordinary a moment
To reveal itself
As the extraordinary

Sydney Weaber
USAF Academy, CO

Water

i love water.

after all,
isn't it the mistress of our world?
the wife of our bodies?
the kiss of our manifestation?

i drink a lot of water,
i indulge in the beauty and grace.
i inhale water,
like air who inhales water;

and it makes me wonder,
if water has this place in my heart,
will i go with it?
will i be like virginia woolf,
and become water?
will i follow bruce lee's advice,
and become water?

i have these wonders frequently.

take right now, for instance.
i'm writing about it,
yet, my curiosity still isn't fulfilled.
hopefully water is my end, though, in some way.

Mia Soto
Tracy, CA

Carcinization

Tell me about crabs
how it always comes back to them
down to them
scurrying across the sand

They've been here longer than most anything
coming and going on and off the water
will my fingers scuttle along
a billion years from now
on grains filed off the memory of our mountains?

I think our fleshy softness
must be the outlier
and if there is a god who made us,
we earthlings,
in their image,
God must be a crab;
and we are just what happens
in the middle
of carcinization.

Aurora Gabow
Denver, CO

Beautiful Demise

Imprinted upon
Sired to
You sank your teeth in
And I wanted you to
You bite woman after woman
Their blood you lust
Because the blood from one person
Is never enough
I'm in love with my captor
His grip is tight
The sun was my life
Now I shield myself from the light
But do I truly love you
Or has your compulsion convinced me to
Are you a predator in the night
Or are you my savior from this life
So many thoughts
Are running through my mind
Which I am starting to believe
Your telepathy helps you find
What is real, what is me
Or do I completely cease to be
As the night closes in
And the dawn draws near
The lines seem to blur
When it comes to fear

Staci Sanders
Toledo, OH

Remember Me

here we are
once again
when I was young
and you seemed old
years go by
so I am told
well here I am
not young but old
for here I stand
once again
to tell you now
as the stories told
young to old
life goes on
it's merry way
and so I go
another way
I leave my gift
from me to you
the gift of love
from me to you
for once i'm gone
this gift I give
will see you through

Kim Stallins
Homosassa, FL

This poem was dedicated to my mother just before her passing. After reading it she cried; this is how I know she loved it. Not only that, but anything that comes from the heart is deeply treasured.

Heavenly Father

From the beginning in the womb of my mother
I was chosen by a loving spirit who would
not give up on me.

He allowed me to live my own life
filled with the void I felt inside, yet all along His
angels were watching over me.

I searched and searched for happiness
to fill my hollow emptiness.

Yet what was missing all along was my Lord Jesus.
I accepted Him inside my heart; He then began to mold
His child whom He created from the start.

Heavenly Father who sacrificed His Son to bring us to
His kingdom. You never have to feel alone; call out to
Jesus and you will be filled with His Holy Spirit.

Elizabeth Blankenship
El Paso, TX

"Heavenly Father" was originally written as a song, sung by me. All that's written in this poem is from my heart. All my life since I was a child my heart felt empty. I would fill my void with things that only brought heartache. I hope this poem touches others and to believe that the Holy Spirit will help and comfort their heart.

Lights, Camera, Dance!

Entering stage ignites a spark
Glowing joyfully in my heart
In a flash, it lights up my soul
No longer in the shadows' hold

With an effulgent grin
The joy radiates from within
Through an elegant twirl
The joy beams out to the world

Around my flowing skirt
A breeze floats and swirls
Spiraling up my body to raise
My spirits high with grace

So buoyant as I share
This joy dancing in the air
May the light of happiness
Illuminate your darkness

Alice Qiao
Redwood City, CA

The Attention Wall

How are you today? I ask every day.
As for I don't know what else to say.
You walk past me in the hall, don't ask me to the ball.
I may as well be the wall
that you give more attention to.
What a shame, the fact that you forget my name.
Even though all your days are the same.
I quest to hear your name.
But not telling me is a greater pain.
Yet you do not know.
I want to hear but it is unclear.
Whether you like me, or not.
You say you like me my mind is in knots.
Yet all of the signs say you don't.
So STOP poisoning me and give me the antidote.
You see I've memorized your schedule,
your birthday, and your street.
I memorized the essay that you presented last week.
But you don't know my name, that's the main pain.
But whatever he's so vain,
just give me the bottle of champagne.
That'll wash away all the pain.
I'll ditch all my human qualities just to be a wall.
A wall you'll give more attention to.

Kierra Van Huyssteen
Reno, NV

Fading

Eyes heavy,
Heart, too.
Mind busy,
Quiet, too.

Shh keep going.
It's okay,
Let them go.
Can't hold on,
Not mine *amour*.

That smell...
Doesn't linger.
What's shared
Returned...almost
Still speak, don't hear
Still listen, hush now.

Stop. Please. Heal. But... No.

Savanna Willauer
Scranton, PA

Faded

I told the moon about you.
And maybe it's because she never answered before
that I don't worry when she remains—
still and silent, never finding me.
I told her of your heart and your mind.
And it would have been so perfect
in her light if she hadn't fallen.
So, I told the sun about you.
And maybe it's because I was so used to the moon's
indifference that I found myself surprised.
For the sun was much brighter than the moon had been.
I mentioned the touch of your fingers
and the hue of your blush.
And perhaps that was enough to please her,
because she did not fade.
It was only when I told her of your fears
born from a void
—of the space
that I found myself once again sharing with the moon.
But she wasn't alone, not like nights before.
So I didn't talk to the moon about you;
instead she talked to me.
And maybe it was the stars that told me to listen.

Lillian Miller
Harbor Springs, MI

Smile

I smile_ I do_ Guess what_You should smile, too
Why?
Because it may just be a smile
To catch you as you fall.
It may just be a smile to shatter down your wall.
1 of the 4 walls that has you currently boxed.
It may just be a smile that shatters all the locks.
Now leaving an open space
For you to crawl out and see.
That giving up isn't the way.
Give hope to possibilities.
It may just be a smile
To save you from that place.
It may just be a smile
That touchless warm embrace.
Yes a smile, a simple smile,
May be exactly what one needs
To step away from the brink
Of ending this life we see.
So be kind,
Take the time to go the extra mile.
Next time you're out
Look upon a random person
And smile

Edna Diaz
Cedarville, NJ

Veterans Day

Land of the free
Because of the brave,
That's why my Ol' Glory flag waves.
Freedom isn't free.
Some need to think about that.
The ones who stayed behind and sat
While others hoped and prayed their loved ones would come back.
Life as an army wife was scary.
The weight of the world on my husband's shoulders, he still has to carry.
Years later,
Still sleepless nights because of nightmares.
Some fears are much greater.
The things he's seen,
The places he's been,
Things he had to do
So we wouldn't have to.
Stood against old and young,
Face to face while holding guns
So you can run around having your fun.
The people you need to hate aren't the ones keeping you safe.
Thank a veteran every day not just today.
These people are giving their lives away
Just so you can say thank you for one day?

Nichole Barnard
Jackson, MO

What about Tomorrow

To what I know, I can attest.
That what I owe, I borrow
From time, without such last request,
As what about tomorrow.

From your caress might I endue
To acquiesce love's powers.
And have each second, spent with you,
Be thereby beckoned hours.

If all before is all there was
With nothing more hereafter,
Then I regret its end because
I'll not forget your laughter.

And if I'm wrong in what I feel
And all along mistaken,
Then let the morning light reveal,
What was forlorn, forsaken.

Thomas Pazur
Aurora, IL

Victory on the Eleventh

It was meant to be fun, actually, that's a lie.
It was a sin birthed from curiousity,
Then, fueled with ignorance, at first.
As I grew, it grew, and I didn't know
That this familiar sin was death in disguise.

I was clueless, but that's no excuse.
For as I grew, I also grew in His Word.
So, I recognized its true identity, and mine as well.
It was a darkness that wrapped itself in pleasure;
A pleasure that made me blind...

Blind, to see what it was taking away from me!
My time, calling, purpose, health and all.
But, I wasn't that blind, nor was I that deaf, to hear.
Hear what He, the Holy Spirit, was saying.
So why didn't I fight it, and just gave myself to it?

I guess I had forgotten my identity as light...
Who shouldn't dwell in the dark, and be defeated by it.

A secret sin on the tenth, but He was there, with me.
On the eleventh, I decided to embrace my identity;
Reporting my sin from the dark to the light.
And His light, I now crave to remain in.
For the light always called, I just chose to be deaf.

Fisayo Odozie
Fresno, CA

Thnx Martin

Let my children judge by their characters,
Not by their titles, wealth, or fame.
For true beauty lies within their hearts,
And not in the facade of their name.
Let them be known for their kindness,
For the love that they freely share.
Let their actions speak louder than words,
And their virtues beyond compare.
Let my daughters judge by their grace,
For their strength and resilience
Is what truly makes them rare.
Let my sons judge by their honor,
Not by the conquests they've made.
For their integrity and bravery,
Their character will forever be their reality trade.

Let my children judge by their voices,
Not by the color of their skin.
Diversity makes us stronger,
And their uniqueness is no sin.
Let them measure by their compassion,
Their empathy and understanding.
For it is how we treat others
That truly defines our standing.
Let my children judge by their characters,
For that is all that truly matters.
When everything else fades away,
Their true selves will still radiate like a lighthouse in tatters.

Darryl K. Porter
Chicago, IL

Fear and Sadness, Those Dastardly Humours

Fear and sadness, those dastardly humours
Slish and slosh within my stomach
And drive me to vomit

Like diseased pumice they ooze
From my skin. From my skin!
And coat my clothes in filth

They soak my bones till waterlogged
I can no longer stand, no longer sing
My throat is caked in phlegm

I feel them in the creases
The crevices of my brain
My head is full of mucus, full of rot

Oh! To open my skull and scrub
Scrub and scrub as a desperate housewife
Against the decay that encroaches her home

Though, it would never be enough
Fear and sadness, those dastardly humours
I will never feel clean again

Zachary Ford
Marianna, FL

For anyone who might be worried, I took a shower after writing this and felt much better. How sweet indeed to be washed in the blood of my King!

Baby Dragon Does a Lifetime

I call myself back from all places,
from across ancient times,
whirling and lost in some nameless desert,
stubbornly kicking through dunes.
My only companions the bottomless struggle,
the constant, restless movement, and
the ache of no destination, no memories of home.

Ah, come away from there now
and wipe your feet, child!
Before you track your stardust
all over my clean galaxy.

I call myself back,
with a voice so gentle and smooth,
lest the tone send me running,
because God knows, she'll run.
Come back, we coax gently, more like a purr,
take a seat here with us;
it's soft, and you can rest.
Holding our breath that
some sudden sound won't send you scurrying,
some inconvenience send you reeling,
away and out of sight again before we could think,
like she was never here at all!
Only angels move that fast.

Michelle Kebabjian
Napa, CA

Thank you, God, thank you Mom & Dad, thank you Maegan, Joel & the kids,
and thank you, Peter. I love you all very, very much.

Memories of the Past

Memories of the past that haunt my soul
I tried to forget it I tried to run away from it
But it stays in my heart taunting me
Every day and night, especially in my dreams
Why won't these feelings end. Is it all in my head
You said you felt what I felt; you said when I hurt you hurt
You said, I was always going to be yours and that you're mine
I didn't believe in us back then
Then you called me your friend
But now years later our friendship has come to an end
Am I supposed to just walk away from you now
How do I end the emptiness in my heart
I should have listened to my head and just let go of the happiness I
can't forget.

Angelique Laqua
Huntington Station, NY

Bright Side

I've been searching for the bright side,
but I've been blinded by the dark,
scouring the cracks and aches of a broken heart.
I'm trying to find the perfect pieces,
to fill these growing holes;
time is never on my side when I need it most.
I've been looking for some answers,
wishing for some change,
hoping to put it back together if I rearrange.
Tripping over fallen hope,
swimming through anxieties,
navigating pain and loss that drown me in their seas.
Staring at these blueprints
and tracing rigid walls,
reaching for the light inside that burnt out long ago.
Writing down the steps to take,
stairs that still need build,
the gravity inside of me has shifted to a tilt.
I've been searching for the bright side,
wandering my way through the dark,
fabricating my dream home
from the shards of a broken heart.

Alexandria Swope
Painsville, OH

Brown Sugar Cane

Your supple skin emanates a sunlit glow,
Captivating eyes, piercing and bold,
With the power to seize one's soul.
Your silhouette, a curvaceous "S," slender and sleek,
Yet behind that innocent and sweet facade,
A fierce lioness resides, untamed, and free.
Your voice, a soothing balm that mends and heals me.
I watch you with longing gaze,
Lost in daydreams of closeness,
Your drive, determination, and unwavering zeal
Inspire and ignite me in ways I can't conceal.
Fear of rejection holds my words at bay,
Hoping one day, my voice won't fail.

Tanishia Bennett
Tacoma, WA

I am honored to be considered as one of 2023 best poets. I would like to thank Jeremiah and Josiah. I thank God for blessing me with this wonderful gift, to be able to artistically express myself.

Just When

Just when I thought
I couldn't breathe
You blew
life
into me

When my eyes
Couldn't see
You said
Open

When my frame was so weak
That I could not stand
You!
Were my pillar of
Strength

And when I was ready to
Give up and
Give in

You said
Not yet!

And so I
Live

Muriel Tolerico
Wickenburg, AZ

I love poetry! Writing poetry opens up a portal of love. It gives me the opportunity to heal and provide sacred ground where others can come purge and heal.

What I Can See

As I walk closer to the gates I stop,
A feeling overtakes me.
A voice like no other rings out,
"Welcome home my daughter."
The gates begin to swing open,
They look as though they weigh a thousand pounds,
But still move as light as a feather.
I am greeted by an old friend,
Then one lady takes me in her arms.
"It's finally nice to meet you face to face."
As my friend leads me down the streets of gold,
She says,"I am so happy you are finally home."
She leads me to place that no words can describe,
There He is.
The man who died to save me,
I see His hands, His side, and His feet.
I fall on my face before Him,
He welcomes me with open arms.
So just imagine what I can see,
One day you will join me.
I am patiently waiting for your arrival,
Together we will tread these streets of gold.
Forever praising our Savior and King.
Death is only a doorway,
And for us it leads to only greater things.
So just try to imagine what I can see.

Kassidy Knight
Dothan, AL

God's Throne

There's no other higher place that you can be heard.
It's spoken and written all throughout God's word.
For when you take your problems there, leave them at his feet.
He will hear you and answer you for the solution you seek.
It may not always be in the answers that you sought.
But it's a God sized problem,
So it's a God's sized solution he has brought.

Michelle Jones
Greenwood, AR

I Love You

How to say I love you
when love is a red rose,
and red is the color of a broken heart.
How to say I love you
when love is a flame,
the flame of a candle put out in an instant.
How to say I love you
when love is a poem,
the poem you never take the time to read.
How to say I love you
when our love is an Icarus
who flew too close then drowned in a sea of loneliness.

Summer Heringer
Mapleton, UT

Golden

Putting God over everything is golden.
Being in your right mind is golden.
Having food, shelter, and clothing is golden.
Having a good portion of your health
and strength is golden.
Having a good supportive inner-
circle is golden.
Having a good source of income is golden.
Having perfect peace in every area of
your life is golden.
To celebrate yourself because you have
life is golden.
Living out God's purpose and
assignment for why he created you
is golden.
Having a good sense of humor during
perilous times is golden.

Tim Austin
Taylor, MI

*I take great dignity in my Christian faith, as well as my African-American culture
which I believe makes that an informing source for the arts which is my poetry
blended with the harlem renaissance, motown, black culture, and the historical
development of blacks. I embrace it. It's a ministry for me. One sound! One rhythm!
One rhyme! One format! A stream of consciousness. A raise of consciousness. As I
was in what I call the dark room—the place where imagination meets creativity
and you always win. I was reflecting on a song entitled "Golden" by Jill Scott. I
decided to take the principles of the song and create my own version as a poem. The
premise is connected to the words in the song that says living life like it's golden.*

O Country Mine

A requiem I sing to thee O Country Mine
As ye sadly sink into a socialistic decline
Gone are the days when work was the answer
A gift for the vote became the cancer
That ate away your founder's vision
Of a republic without division
So many died to keep you strong
The office seeker made it all go wrong
Taxes and electees destroyed the makers
And you were inundated with the takers
Why should they work when it could all be free
So they voted in mass for that nominee
Generations will be burdened by the spending spree
Until you collapse into anarchy
A requiem I sing to thee O Country Mine
History will remember you, a nation divine.

Joseph Maxwell White
Williamsburg, VA

Mighty Wings

When you feel weariness, distress
and need of rest
Just lift your wings
and you'll be blessed

For you will soar upward
upward...upward today
if you lift your wings
Christ will lead the way
for you can be lifted
emotionally, spiritually
this very hour

just whisper that "Name"
the name of the one who
has the power

And, put all your faith in
the strength God brings

the Authority!
to lift your mighty wings!

Helen Roark
Beckley, WV

In Reality

In reality I pray for God to guide my
ink pen as I write day or night. When
I'm weary I love rest! I'm down sizing
my place of "30 years" because of the
needed repairs. In reality I awake
from strange dreams of people and places,
and certain things of long ago. In reality
to downsize I find forgotten letters and
photos of folks I used to know. We need
concerns of favorite photos and such
rather than certain replaceable items
we hold onto so much. For my 76th
birthday my photo was on a TV list
for birthdays and it was nice! I had a
lovely Thanksgiving and Christmas, too. One
gift was a small wheel chair to assist
when I go to a mall or parade or such.
It helped at a procession so much! By
a surprise I was interviewed by a 1st
News Place. By evening and p.m. I was
informed it went worldwide. (If I win
a big lottery I can publish my true
life in privacy. It's suggested.) As
a teen I was on a "missing" poster of
my home state. It's suggested it will be
a best seller! At times I attended some
churchs where folks would sing and shout.
Perhaps in reality someone will benefit
in decisions—there's no doubt!

Frances Elaine Camp
Americus, GA
*I'm getting older and realize I'm no spring chicken anymore! I don't sew or type or
take long walks as I used to. Except a Walmart cart can pull me forward as I go! I've
considered Ohio as my first home. I was born there... and I've considered Georgia
my second home. I got a new karaoke machine for Christmas 2023. My heart and
part youthful memories remain in Ohio where elderly precious folks were.*

When Our First Kiss Up to the Heavens Soared

[Dedicated to Angel]

When our first kiss up to the heavens soared,
An ardent passion swirled around the air.
With no sense of time—neither her nor there—
A bond was formed, and faith in love restored.

With the kind permission of the good Lord,
Our lips softly met with the upmost care.
I gently ran my fingers through your hair
To ensure you felt treasured and adored.

As we held each other in our embrace,
Our frames began to feel dizzy and weak—
We felt the work of a higher power.

Once we separated, I touched your face,
Running my hand down the side of your cheek—
Your warm skin felt tender as a flower.

Making sadness cower,
Our eternal love then began showing—
And both of our faces kept on glowing.

We parted, both knowing
The night can be cold in so many ways—
But the warmth of our kiss lasted for days.

Thomas Koron
DeKalb, IL

I have always had a strong passion for poetry. I believe that it is more than just words on a page, and it ultimately has the power to change our lives. I am particularly fond of the works of Edgar Allan Poe, William Shakespeare, John Keats, Robert Browning, Christina Rossetti, William Wadsworth, Samuel Taylor Coleridge, Percy Bysshe Shelley and Lord Byron. All of their poetry is powerfully written in their own unique voices. Reading their work has definitely had a profound impact on me as a writer. My favorite poetic forms include the sonnet, the villanelle, and the dramatic monologue.

Thoughts

Where do thoughts go when they leave the mind?
If thoughts are not written down and not captured on paper,
they disappear.
Imagine if thoughts were words or sentences
or paragraphs or stories or chapters written down.
There would not be enough bookshelves in libraries around the world
to contain such volumes of thoughts.
It is a wonder how thoughts come and go.
Most thoughts are of the past and most thoughts are of the future
but few thoughts are really of the present moment.
Thoughts are of judgment.
Thoughts are of good intentions.
Thoughts are thoughts of feelings.
Thoughts are the babbling mind trying to take center stage of one's life.
Thoughts are of avoidance to survive the loneliness of the mind.
Thoughts are of control.
Thoughts are of survival.
Thoughts block out uncomfortableness and uncertainty.
Thoughts can be a bad neighborhood in the wrong part of town.
Thoughts can be the mind's best friend.
Thoughts can go deep in the psyche.
Thoughts can slide across the surface.
Thoughts can come and go quicker than the blink of the eye.
Thoughts have no sound but can be louder than
the biggest boom ever heard.
Thoughts can be quiet and give the effect of peace and serenity.
Thoughts are a reality and yet they go unnoticed as if they do not exist.
Where do thoughts go once they leave the mind?

Roger Herbert Dobitz
Sioux City, IA

*Growing up with a hearing loss caused me to go inside of myself to make sense
of living in a world where most people can hear readily and easily. I would write
down what was going on inside of my head. This helped to make sense for me
what I was thinking. When I put my thoughts down on paper; it became real in
my mind. That's why I write. It helps me to be sane and have serenity in my life.*

Hear the Quiet

The river is high
   perfectly still
      grieving the night's storm

Fish bob for insects
   in the murky water's web
      leaving spirals in their wake

Angel hair clouds
     melt in the sky

Forget-me-nots
     lift their wilted heads

Birds mend soggy nests
     conversing in melody

Young poplars shimmer
     in the warm soft wind

A butterfly curtsey's, then blushes
     as a suitor makes himsellf known

A determined dam endures
     after the fateful flood

Vermont flood July of 2024

Corinne Davis
Montpelier, VT

I am the granddaughter of the late Deane C. Davis, Vermont's 74th governor who served from 1969–73, and Corinne Eastman Davis (1901–51). Granddaughter and namesake I'm in the process of writing the last chapter of my grandmother's unfinished manuscript titled Crazy about the Country. *She had won first prize for her novel synopsis of this book awarded by the Vermont Federation of Women's Clubs in 1945. I've changed the title to* Love Song *because it has given me deep insight into my grandparent's love of Vermont and, most of all, for one another.*

Next Generation, Follow This Trail

Inflaming the expectations for the future
Is what historic American trails do.
Since there are so many, not just a few,
Let us concentrate on one to review,
Located in Hopkinsville, Kentucky, no doubt.
The burial site for Cherokee chiefs two,
For much more we find facts about
How they and thousands more on this Trail of Tears
Came with disease, little sanitation and fears.
We know these chiefs, the evidence of which grew.
Names were Fly Smith and Whitepath
Which with modern names might bring a laugh.
In 1987 when President Reagan signed a bill
Creating this as a national historic trail
Many would remember without fail
That not much along this site brought a thrill.
Statues of these Cherokee men
Were crafted by Steve Smith, remembered *now* and *then*.
Red Cherokee Dogwoods are here for clans to revere.
Paint, Bird, Blue, Wolf, Long Hair, Wild Potato, Deer.
For them, we shed many a tear.
Recalling how this trail came to be
With forced removal of the Cherokee
To Indian territory known now as Oklahoma state.
A lesson we learn is no hate
On what happened there, is not for *debate*.

Bobbie Jean Burnett
Russellville, KY

Since childhood, I have dreamed of being an author. When my husband died, I decided to fulfil that dream. My first book Memories of My Addiction *was published in March 2023 and my second book* Kentucky Keepsakes *was published in January 2024. the both include a captivating compilation of memories through short stories and poetry. In the second book there is a special section featuring writings which I assisted former students of grades four through eight during Kentucky's mandates of writing portfolios.*

Prospect High School

I want my time back
the time you stole with your obtuse conclusions
deeming my symptoms mere delusions
but don't worry, I did learn something
when you forced my aching body to class
I learned that my life meant nothing to you
if I couldn't appease your standards and pass

You stole my years of teenage youth
forced me to believe bare minimum accommodations
were special gifts, difficult tasks, and rare salvations
stranding me in remote anguish
begging to be sane, blaming myself for my pain

How dare you tell me I was too young to be sick?
How dare you penalize me for your inadequacy?
How dare you not lift a finger when I withdrew?

I know why, now that it's too late
Because I was getting rid of your burden
the burden you taught me I was
I could have thrived, oh how I would've thrived
Could've made memories at prom
Could've graduated with my friends
Could've flourished, learned, and seen it through
Now I know the fault never lay within me...but in you

Yoselynn Tavares
Mount Prospect, IL

*I often wonder who I could've been had I known my school wasn't doing everything
they could. If I didn't have to withdraw from public school because it was too
inaccessible. If my grades weren't penalized for missing class because I'd fainted,
if my symptoms were taken seriously instead of downgraded. My chronic illness
isn't what stole my time. Uneducated school systems focused on producing abled
and exceptional cogs in the societal machine inherently designed without disabled
students in mind stole it.*

The Tale of the Cardboard Boat

We started to build a boat
Mommy and Daddy and me were there
Just cardboard, duct tape, and paint
The rules were pretty clear.

Daddy got all the stuff
Most of what was required
We all painted and taped the cardboard
We worked until we were tired.

The boat turned out pretty good
We were pleased as punch
My mommy, my daddy and me
We were a proud and happy bunch.

We took that boat to the campground
And launched it on the pond
Mommy got it all in pictures
While Daddy and me rowed and won.

Daddy paddled while I steered
And kept that boat afloat
We sailed away and made it back
Us and our cardboard boat.

Bonnie Jean Houghton
Owego, NY

After working forty-eight years, I am a retired accountant from two major US government defense contractors. I've worked as a child assigned aide at a local elementary school and I have also retired after nine years from being a socal welfare examiner from our county department of social services. I am the mother of three great and successful sons and their spouses and the grandmother of seven wonderful grandchildren. I never started to write poetry until after the death of my mother but now enjoy it most when writing for special occasions for close friends and family. This has been a dream for me to have one book published of my very own. I have been so greatly blessed by my heavenly Father for all I've been given in my life.

Halloween's Trick-or-Treat Surprise

Bright yellow birch leaves fall floating in wind songs;
They dance in leaps, lifts and dives.
Oak leaves catch the wind,
Red brown leaf palms,
They dive to the ground and hold in tight bond.
Golden yellow maple leaves fall all together,
Hands reaching out in leaf family groups.
They gather in layers forming maple blankets,
Spread across mattresses of green grassy ground.
Fall falls in multicolored adornments,
Painting autumn personalities
Across lawns, woods, and fields.
They are the last sentences of Summer's goodbye letter.
Halloween brings us a northern cold surprise.
I stand behind tall patio door windows,
Watching wind whip and swirl new cold, white, snow
Coating lawns, coating trees,
Covering all of your gardens and flowers.
Halloween's trick or treat speaks its first message,
A letter of its promises yet to come.
I see hidden stories in swirling snow's design.
You stand beside me wondering at winter's white beauty.
In a world full of so much uncertainty
And unanswered questions,
Halloween's magic snowfall brings us the beauty
Of this Halloween's trick or treat surprise.

Greg Bass
Pleasant Prairie, WI

As a poet my development of voice has been a continued development of poetic style. My continued and constant effort is to use the integration of our relationship between environmental truth and poetic aesthetic to build metaphor and analogy. The metaphor and analogy are constructs of the underlying imagery message that is my poem's purpose. My commitment to voice development has taken many paths and studies, including graduate work in and MFA, MDiv, and studying modern American poets. I also have done extensive study of my environmental heroes John Muir and Aldo Leopold. Truth is, there is never a complete end to finding voice and the evolution of style. Life changes, change voice.

Winter Storm

Winter is here the trees are all bare
The leaves have fallen to the ground
A chilling breeze is in the air
Cold winds are southern bound

Ice has come with the freezing rain
Making everything appear glass
The newsman says watch for a change
A blizzard is coming in fast

The freezing wind blows around us
Making shivers run up our spine
We should not have treaded out in this
But the car wouldn't move from the drive

The storm is now calming
It's clearing enough to see
But not enough for walking
So homebound we will be

Patty Smith
Clinton, IA

Index of Poets